Wooden Spoon
ANNIVERSARY

RUGBYWORLD
Yearbook 2009

Editor

Ian Robertson

Photographs

Getty Images

GreenUmbrella
Publishing

This book has been produced for Green Umbrella Publishing
by Lennard Books
a division of Lennard Associates Ltd
Windmill Cottage
Mackerye End
Harpenden
Herts AL5 5DR

© Lennard Associates Limited 2008

This edition first published in the UK in 2008
by Green Umbrella Publishing

www.gupublishing.co.uk

Paperback   ISBN 978 1 906635 21 3
Hardback   ISBN 978 1 906635 22 0

Production Editor: Chris Marshall
Design Consultant: Paul Cooper
Jacket Design: Kevin Gardner
Printed and bound in Slovenia

The publishers would like to thank Getty Images for providing most of the photographs for this book. The publishers would also like to thank Fotosport UK, Inphopics, Chris Thau and Wooden Spoon for additional material.

The views in this book are those of the author but they are general views only and readers are urged to consult the relevant and qualified specialist for individual advice in particular situations.

OFFICIAL
BEER

ENGLAND
RUGBY

Greene King IPA
Britain's favourite cask beer

GREENE KING
IPA
nothing to prove

PASSION, DETERMINATION AND SUCCESS

Travis Perkins

PROUD SPONSORS OF THE NORTHAMPTON SAINTS

Travis Perkins is the UK's leading builders merchant and supplies more than 100,000 product lines to the trade, including:

- General building materials
- Plumbing and heating
- Landscaping materials
- Timber and sheet materials
- Painting and decorating
- Drylining and insulation
- Tool and equipment hire
- Doors and joinery
- Bathrooms and kitchens
- Hand and power tools

Contents

Foreword by HRH The Princess Royal   7

Wooden Spoon: In the Beginning ... (Julian Crabtree)   8

COMMENT & FEATURES
Jus Summum Sæpe Summa Est Malitia (Paul Stephens)   16
Geech Goes Back: the 2009 Lions Tour to South Africa (Mick Cleary)   22
Golden Centenary: 100 Years of Wallaby Touring (Chris Thau)   27

INTERNATIONAL SCENE
Robbie Deans: Teambuilding Beyond the Tasman (Raechelle Inman)   32
Forging Ahead: A Revolution in German Rugby (Chris Thau)   38
Passion and Talent: Looking to the Future in the Pacific (Raechelle Inman)   42
Sons of the Sun: Georgian Rugby on the Rise (Chris Thau)   48
Kiwis Lead the Field: the 2008 Junior World Championship (Alan Lorimer)   52
International Sevens:
        Hong Kong: Rock 'n' Roll Rugby (Rebecca Butler)   58
        Dubai: Tomorrow the World (Cup) (Rebecca Butler)   64
Summer Tours 2008:
        England in New Zealand (Steve Bale)   68
        Scotland in Argentina (Alan Lorimer)   72
        Wales in South Africa (Graham Clutton)   76
        Ireland Down Under (Sean Diffley)   81
        Churchill Cup (Hugh Godwin)   84

HOME FRONT
Wasps Dig Deep: the 2007-08 Guinness Premiership (Chris Hewett)   91
Farewell the Warrior: What Now for Lawrence Dallaglio? (Chris Jones)   97
Munster Turn the Tide: the 2008 Heineken Cup Final (Alastair Hignell)   101
The Return of Bath: the 2008 Challenge Cup Final (Terry Cooper)   108

REVIEW OF THE SEASON 2007-08
Grand Slam Gatland: the 2008 Six Nations Championship (Chris Jones)   114
The Club Scene:
        England: An Up-and-Down Year (Bill Mitchell)   119
        Scotland: Robinson's Revolution (Alan Lorimer)   123
        Wales: EDF Not Enough for Ospreys (David Stewart)   128
        Ireland: A Topsy-Turvy Season (Sean Diffley)   132
        France: Spirit Burns Hot at Toulouse (Chris Thau)   135
        Italy: Calvisano Reach the Top (Chris Thau)   138
A Summary of the Season 2007-08 (Terry Cooper)   140

PREVIEW OF THE SEASON 2008-09
Key Players 2008-09 (Ian Robertson)   150
Fixtures 2008-09   156

WOODEN SPOON TOUR

The best value tour for Spoon supporters

British & Irish Lions Tour

South Africa 2009

Follow the Lions on the Spoon Tour

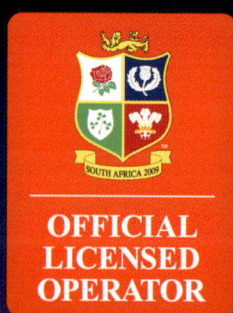

OFFICIAL LICENSED OPERATOR

Your itinerary

18 Jun	Depart **UK**	
19-22 Jun	**Durban**	Three nights at Westville Boutique Guest House and Manors
22-26 Jun	**Cape Town**	Four nights at Southern Sun Cullinan
26-30	**Johannesburg**	Four nights at The Westcliffe Hotel
30 Jun-2 Jul	**North West Province (Safari)**	Two nights at Madikwe River & Safari Lodge
2-5 Jul	**Johannesburg**	Three nights at Protea Hotel Melrose
5 Jul	Depart **Johannesburg**	
6 Jul	**Arrive UK**	From £5,745 per person

Costs include

- ✓ Direct flights Heathrow/Johannesburg on South African Airways
- ✓ Hotels on B&B basis
- ✓ Full board on safari with four game drives
- ✓ Official match tickets: 3 Tests (Durban, Pretoria, Johannesburg) and provincial match against Emerging Springboks (face value cost extra)
- ✓ Entry to Gullivers exclusive Big Pubs at Test Matches
- ✓ Entry to Gullivers exclusive Wine Festival
- ✓ Transfers
- ✓ Official Gullivers Merchandise (supplied by adidas)
- ✓ Gullivers Tour Manager

Wooden Spoon Registered Charity No 326691

Special features

Wooden Spoon, jointly with South African Rugby Legends offers

- ✓ Two Black Tie Dinners with members of the South African and Lions squads
- ✓ Two Golf Days: Durban Country Club and Royal Johannesburg.
- ✓ Gullivers contribution to Wooden Spoon for every booking

Peace of mind with Gullivers

- • Official travel and match tickets
- • Fully licensed tour operator
- • The UK's leading and longest established rugby tour operator

For further information, please contact Gullivers and quote **'Spoon Tour'**

HSBC

PRINCIPAL PARTNER

For further information and brochures, please visit
www.gulliverstravel.co.uk Or call us on

01684 293175

Gullivers
sports travel

FOREWORD

by HRH THE PRINCESS ROYAL

BUCKINGHAM PALACE

The game of rugby has changed much over the last 25 years but the one constant factor in this development of the game has been the continuing growth and effectiveness of Wooden Spoon, the Charity of British and Irish rugby.

Wooden Spoon was founded after England's disappointment on the rugby pitch in 1983. Since then, Spoon has gone from strength to strength investing many resources into easing the hardships of children and young people disadvantaged in life.

Rugby is a game of great commitment requiring energy, enthusiasm and skill that are translated into a physically demanding and invariably exciting spectacle. The volunteers, members and supporters of Wooden Spoon bring the same attributes to their fundraising activities for the benefit of others.

As Wooden Spoon celebrates its 25th anniversary, we can look back with immense pride at its achievements and growth and in particular the number of children whose lives have been impacted because of the work of the Charity.

I wish everyone involved with Wooden Spoon success with their fundraising during this celebratory year and thank you for supporting a Charity that does so much to reflect the finest team game in the world.

Anne

HRH The Princess Royal,
Royal Patron of Wooden Spoon.

Wooden Spoon

ANNIVERSARY

In the Beginning ...

by JULIAN CRABTREE

Royal Patron: HRH The Princess Royal
Patrons: Rugby Football Union • Scottish Rugby Union
                  Welsh Rugby Union • Irish Rugby Football Union

In an age when the spirit of sport is often called into question and winning at all costs seems to be the norm, Wooden Spoon can look back with huge pride on their success, which was born from a loss in the sporting arena. Strangely enough the man who set the Wooden Spoon wheels in motion only recently discovered his part in the formation of rugby's charity. That man was Ireland fly half Ollie Campbell, whose try, conversion and five penalty goals saw England lose 25-15 in

IRELAND		ENGLAND
H. P. MacNEILL BLACKROCK COLLEGE	**15**	**W. H. HARE** LEICESTER
T. M. RINGLAND BALLYMENA	**14**	**J. CARLETON** ORRELL
D. G. IRWIN INSTONIANS	**13**	**C. R. WOODWARD** LEICESTER
M. J. KIERNAN DOLPHIN	**12**	**P. W. DODGE** LEICESTER
M. C. FINN CORK CONSTITUTION	**11**	***D. TRICK** BATH
S. O. CAMPBELL OLD BELVEDERE	**10**	**J. P. HORTON** BATH
R. J. M. McGRATH WANDERERS	**9**	**N. C. YOUNGS** LEICESTER
W. P. DUGGAN BLACKROCK COLLEGE	**8**	**J. P. SCOTT** CAPTAIN CARDIFF
J. B. O'DRISCOLL MANCHESTER	**7**	**P. J. WINTERBOTTOM** HEADINGLEY
J. F. SLATTERY BLACKROCK COLLEGE	**6**	**N. C. JEAVONS** MOSELEY
M. I. KEANE LANSDOWNE	**5**	**S. BAINBRIDGE** GOSFORTH
D. G. LENIHAN CORK CONSTITUTION	**4**	**S. B. BOYLE** GLOUCESTER
G. A. J. McLOUGHLIN SHANNON	**3**	**G. S. PEARCE** NORTHAMPTON
CAPTAIN **C. F. FITZGERALD** ST. MARY'S COLLEGE	**2**	**P. J. WHEELER** LEICESTER
P. A. ORR OLD WESLEY	**1**	**C. E. SMART** NEWPORT

Replacements:	Replacements:
16 M. P. Fitzpatrick (Wanderers)	16 N. C. Stringer (Wasps)
17 J. L. Cantrell (Blackrock College)	17 G. H. Davies (Coventry)
18 C. C. Tucker (Shannon)	18 S. J. Smith (Sale)
19 M. T. Bradley (Cork Constitution)	19 P. A. G. Rendall (Wasps)
20 A. J. P. Ward (St. Mary's College)	20 S. G. F. Mills (Gloucester)
21 J. J. Murphy (Greystones)	21 R. Hesford (Bristol)

Dublin in 1983 and despatched them to the bottom of the Five Nations table into the bargain.

It was a tough day for England, especially debutant David Trick, who was not only playing out of position but has also been blamed for dropping Campbell's massive up-and-under, which resulted in his try. 'Yes, of course everyone remembers that dropped ball,' sighs Trick. 'But I always maintain that in order to drop a ball you actually have to touch it. Let's just say that my first touch of the ball in international rugby was when that ball bounced through my arms and caught me in the bollocks on the way up. I got absolutely mullered by the Irish pack, they steamrolled over me and spat me out the back end of the ruck.'

Campbell, described by prop Ginger McLoughlin as the greatest player he ever played with, in any position, bar none, has very fond memories of the game but was not aware of the part he played. 'I did not realise until recently that the match of 1983 was the start of Wooden Spoon,' explained Campbell. 'Obviously I am well aware of the good work that the charity does and am amazed that it started that day.'

The loss was certainly not going to spoil a good night out in Dublin, and five English fans settled in for a meal with some Irish friends. Banter, some fine food and even finer wine was the order of the day. However, just before departure for the airport, the Irish contingent decided that it would be very amusing to present their English guests with a wooden spoon to mark the occasion. To the rousing anthem of 'Three Blind Mice', the spoon was presented, wrapped up in an Irish scarf, on a silver platter. Somehow the spoon ended up on the plane back to Blighty with our intrepid English fans, who insisted that everyone on the flight should sign it, including many of the Irish players, the pilot, Willie John McBride and a pop star's mum!

Back in England, the original group of five – Peter Scott, Steve Scott, Michael Scott, Nigel Timson and Vic Durling – grew as David Roberts, Fred Hucker and Tom Madden got involved. The original idea was to form the Wooden Spoon Golfing Society. However, Fred Hucker was not a golfer and at a very long lunch at Motcombs Restaurant in London, he persuaded the others to drop the word 'golfing' and the Wooden Spoon Society was born.

Golf was still on the agenda, though, and Farnham Golf Club was the venue for the first golf day and rugby supper, where the plan was to invite a few people to play some golf, raise some cash for a charity and have a couple of drinks. 'Golfers went home far too early and we wanted to have a couple of drinks afterwards, so we made it a rugby dinner,' remembers Vic Durling.

The evening was a resounding success. The club ran out of alcohol and had to buy some from a local hotel at 4 am, Barry Cryer wrote a sketch based on two of the guests and by the next morning £8450 had been raised from all sorts of antics and auctions. The money funded the purchase of a minibus for the Park Special Needs School in Aylesbury via the charity Sunshine Coaches. Once the dust had settled, the group reflected on the significant amount raised and how there was potential to help more people while having fun. So the Wooden Spoon Society became a charity.

News of the success of the golf day spread and soon the group were fielding calls from all over the country asking them to organise more. This was tough work. Behind the ideals of having fun while raising money for charity was a lot of planning and organising – all done while holding down full-time jobs or, in Michael Scott's case, still at school. But those early days were vital for Spoon's development and laid down the strong foundations on which the charity is built. Those involved not only made some good money for charities and projects but more importantly forged friendships with companies and individuals that are still going strong today.

After the success of the inaugural golf day, the founders hosted a St George's Dinner at the Rose Room at Twickenham. It was a male-only event for 400 rugby-centric people and was a great success. This then led to the hosting of the first Annual Ball at the Hilton. The overwhelming triumph of this event ensured it became a permanent date in the diary for many Spooners. Over the years the ball has contributed more than £3 million to Spoon.

In between working and raising money, the founders continued to spread the word according to Spoon. They carried on attending rugby matches with their Irish, Scottish, Welsh and French friends and it was this network of rugby fans that built up the charity. The work of Spoon stretched far and wide and soon volunteer committees to assist in organisation and fund-raising sprang up in Wales and the Midlands. Today this volunteer workforce stretches across 43 Regions in the UK and Ireland and is the backbone of the charity.

The impact of what they were doing and how they were changing lives hit home when they presented a medical camera to a professor at Great Ormond Street Hospital during one of their functions. 'He came onto the dance floor and he lost control,' remembers Steve Scott. 'We all sat there thinking "What have we done?" It was an important moment for us, as we saw first hand what an impact we were having.'

Twenty-five years later, Spoon has raised over £14 million to help improve the lives of mentally, physically and socially disadvantaged children and young people in the UK and Ireland. Spoon has funded or part-funded over 275 capital projects, including sensory rooms and gardens, hydrotherapy pools, refuge centres and play areas. These facilities have helped more than 500,000 children – and

their families – who suffer from many disabilities, such as autism, cystic fibrosis and special needs. Other grants have gone towards projects to support socially disadvantaged children and young people, to combat bullying, violence, crime, obesity discrimination and social deprivation.

It has been a great journey for all those who have had the pleasure of being involved with the charity, among them the founders and staff, honorary presidents, corporate supporters, fund-raisers,

members, friends, and of course the volunteers, without whom the charity would not have grown so fast and so successfully. The growth stemmed from the desire to help improve the lives of disadvantaged children. Like-minded individuals found they were happy to get together to show that good sportsmanship could be extended to help others. It almost seemed in those early years as if the more fun people had raising money, the more money was raised – and the more projects Spoon was able to support. It is an ethos that Spoon has carried through to the present day.

Spoon's strength and purpose still remains to convert the funds raised from rugby, fund-raising events and other activities to benefit children and young people disadvantaged in life. Wooden Spoon is driven by a collective ambition to see the charity continue to grow in stature and thereby continue to have a positive impact. The founders are proud of the people who continue to work for Spoon and know that the charity is in good hands. 'As the charity has increased in size, depth and financial return, something different has happened,' explained Fred Hucker. 'That professionalism is something different to what we started, we all recognise that but there are times when we do hark back to the old days.

'However, the good news is that we have done the first 25 years and they will take it on to the next 25 years. We respect that and we understand why the changes have happened and without those changes it would not have grown like it has. We have made the investment and done the fundamentals, now we leave it up to them. That is not to say we are going to disappear, we are simply saying that that is what we were, now it is different.'

Wooden Spoon continues to attract many different characters and it is not difficult to see why. The boldness and belief of the founders has been developed over the years and has created something more than just a charity. It has created a family; a family doing its best to look after each other, to enjoy life and to make the most of opportunities – for ourselves and for one another.

David Trick possibly sums it up best as he remembers his debut with fondness. 'With hindsight I am quite glad that I did have a pretty poor game and England did lose that game,' said Trick. 'Because I cannot envisage five supporters getting together and starting a charity called "Fourth Place" – which is where England would have come if we had won that game. Wooden Spoon has a much better ring to it don't you think?

'I think that the £14 million that they have raised over the 25 years certainly takes the sting out of a miserable day on the wing.'

Spoon is celebrating its 25th Anniversary over a period of two years. The first year – to March 2009 – will be known as the Founders' Year and will celebrate the formation of the charity and the past 25 years. From March 2009 to March 2010, it will be celebrating the future – the next 25 years – and laying the foundations for the next phase in the charity's history.

There is a natural theme for the two years of celebrations – 25. Spoon's target is to raise £2.5 million over the two-year period, to create 25 new projects, to change the lives of another 250,000 children, to host over 250 fund-raising events each year, to increase membership to 25,000 and to bring on board 25 new sponsors. It will not be easy, but there is nothing stronger than the heart of a volunteer, and Spoon has some of the best in the business working to take the charity to a new level and support more children who need a helping hand in life.

For more details on Wooden Spoon, its 25th Anniversary fund-raising events and activities, visit the website:

www.woodenspoon.com

Ready for a challenge

Breaking through barriers. Investec supports Wooden Spoon.
We thrive on working together with our clients to help them
achieve their goals. Bringing a fresh approach to banking across
a range of specialist services. For more information, call
020 7597 4000 or visit our website **www.investec.com**

Australia • Botswana • Canada • Hong Kong • Ireland • Mauritius • Namibia • South Africa
Switzerland • Taiwan • United Kingdom & Channel Islands • United States

Out of the Ordinary™

Asset Management • Capital Markets • Investment Banking • Private Banking • Property Investments

COMMENT
& FEATURES

Jus Summum Sæpe Summa Est Malitia

by PAUL STEPHENS

'Four players were eventually named in the press in connection with the incidents … all of whom had taken part in the shambolic game, surrendered to the All Blacks 37-20'

Had Victor Meldrew, the hapless hero of the popular television series *One Foot in the Grave*, been in charge of England's summer tour to New Zealand, it would have been no surprise to anyone if they made as many mistakes as they did. But error followed unmistakeable calamity, from the moment the touring party was first announced. It was not that England did not win the two-Test series; very few sides going to New Zealand are able to accomplish that. But what a shambles it was, the England team losing by the second-biggest margin in more than a century.

For many it began with the absence of the latest England golden boy, Danny Cipriani, who suffered a dislocated ankle in a club match and is unlikely to play again until November 2008. With Jonny Wilkinson also facing surgery to his injured shoulder, there were no genuinely worthy first-class outside halves available to take on the estimable Dan Carter. England were faced with the limited choice of Charlie Hodgson, Toby Flood or Olly Barkley. Not that the scrum halves were much better. Richard Wigglesworth, Danny Care and Peter Richards were the chosen trio. Lewis Moody, James Simpson-Daniel, Louis Deacon, Harry Ellis, Simon Shaw, Phil Vickery and Shane Geraghty were among the distinguished cast of absentees.

In case you missed it, there was even greater discontinuity over the role of Brian Ashton, who coached England to the final of the most recent World Cup in France. Where had he gone all of a sudden? There was an unholy fuss from some quarters about the way Ashton was treated by Francis Baron and Rob Andrew, though it soon became clear that Martin Johnson was unhappy working with Ashton, so the little man had to go.

The RFU offered Ashton a job with their academy, but there was no way he was going to accept this, in spite of the RFU's late rejection of claims that they had issued Ashton with an ultimatum to make his mind up before Johnson took over on 1 July and announced his 32-man elite squad together with a Saxons outfit. Ashton has since been appointed a coaching consultant with the RFU, helping coaches and players on a 12-month renewable contract. This cachinnate episode was cack-handed and had all the hallmarks of a soccer plot involving one of the clubs from the lower divisions in the English leagues. More was to follow.

After the Auckland Test, some England players were reported to have entertained a girl in a room at the Hilton Hotel and there were accusations of sexual assault and rape. Another girl went on to reveal a separate encounter with an England player in a British Sunday newspaper. Four players were eventually named in the press in connection with the incidents – David Strettle, Topsy Ojo, Mike Brown and Danny Care – all of whom had taken part in the shambolic game, surrendered to the All Blacks 37-20. The local police were called in, but no charges were brought.

Of the accusations, Johnson said, 'The allegations made against the England team were serious. We cannot have this for our team, for our sport. It is not what we are about. The England team have never had it before and we should never have it again.' Johnson took no part in the New Zealand tour, staying at home to be at the birth of his second child.

Meanwhile, the RFU called on their disciplinary officer, Jeff Blackett QC, to investigate the whole lewd, squalid tale. The rape issue was eventually scotched when confirmation was received from New Zealand that incriminations would not be levied, although solicitor's testimony was laid before

Sex claim England players nam

But official rugby report says there is no evidence of criminal wrongdoing

By Gordon Rayner, Chief Reporter

THREE England players who were accused of sexually abusing a teenage girl during a tour of New Zealand last month have been named in a report by the Rugby Football Union.

Topsy Ojo, Mike Brown and Danny Care were accused by the 18-year-old of "sexually violating" her in a hotel room with a fourth player who has not been named. The four men vehemently deny the allegations.

The report, by the RFU's disciplinary officer, Jeff Blackett, discloses that the teenager made an allegation of "sexual abuse/rape" to police and doctors at a hospital where she sought treatment. Until now, it had been thought that she had refused to confirm an allegation made against the players by her boyfriend.

Solicitors for the girl have told Mr Blackett that she suffered injuries which were "definitely indicative of non-consensual sex". The report says the alleged victim "stands by" the allegation, but "does not want to go through the criminal process".

Because no formal com...

...to a second bar and later to the Pony Club, where Ojo and the girl kissed.

After going on to another club, Brown kissed and danced with the girl, and they left for the team hotel at 7am. The girl went back to Brown's room with him, and at 8.15am Ojo banged on the door to say they had an appointment with the physiotherapist.

The report says that Ojo claims to have stayed in the room on his own with the girl. He later took her to the foyer and she left. Players said she was "not distressed, but a little embarrassed." That day the teenager went to a hospital where doctors treating her injuries referred her to the police.

Mr Blackett says that a police "job sheet" detailing her allegation states that "she consented to going to the hotel room of one of the players; that there was consensual sexual activity with that player; but that three other...

Danny Care
FOOTBALL REJECT

Care was born in Leeds. Aged 11, he joined the academy of Sheffield Wednesday FC as a striker but was told he was too small to hold his own against bigger opponents.

He concentrated on rugby and, after reaching a stocky 5ft 9in, established himself as a tough scrum-half. Care, 21, who plays for the London club Harlequins, made his...

Topsy Ojo
LAW STUDENT

Grammar school-educated Ojo is a law student at Birkbeck

Rampant Rabbit was real tryer

Model tells of star's sex marathon on England rugby's night of shame

Team bussed girls to 'rape claim' hotel

By Lucy Panton & Frank Thorne

THE blonde Alice in Wonderland girl who romped with an England star on rugby's night of shame today lifts the sheets on the rape claim scandal.

Sophie Lewis—pictured here in her party outfit for the first time—sensationally reveals that the "RAMPANT RABBIT" who bedded her at the team hotel was winger David Strettle.

"He pressed all the right buttons and kissed me in all the right places," she says. "He was so energetic."

But Strettle was missing from England's latest humiliating defeat in New Zealand yesterday with a hamstring injury.

The 22-year-old beauty—known as Angel—also tells how players didn't have to sneak girls back from a sleazy club for sex on the night of the alleged rape.

England are told to stop the partying

Party animals perhaps, criminals no

Comment
By Mick Cleary

AND to think that the Rugby Football Union used to insist on their telephone number being ex-directory. No one can accuse them today of a lack of transparency. They promised full disclosure on the murky, muddled events of that long night and steamy morning in Auckland, and they delivered — 14 pages, 7,211 words. That's not the output of a body intent in...

You imagine he would have adopted the same stance even if there had been something unpalatable at the heart of the matter. As it is, the depth and detail of the report casts all four players in a different light to that which they have been forced to endure over the past four weeks. They may have been protected by anonymity for legal reasons but the innuendo has been just as damaging. Party animals, perhaps; criminals, no.

Those close to them wanted to go on the offensive...

rape, for that is what they were effectively accused of, is one of the most heinous in the charge book.

Perhaps now the record can be put in another context, the infractions by Mike Brown and Topsy Ojo notwithstanding. That said, accounts of late-night drinking and dawn returns to hotels is not conduct becoming professional sportsmen.

Blackett will not have gone easy on the players. He may not have subjected them to a bare chair and swinging light...

THE TOUR OF SHAME: JUDGEMENT DAY

Topsy Ojo
REPRIMANDED and fined £500 for staying out all night during England tour. Warned in future not to put **GUILTY**

David Strettle
FOUND not guilty of any misconduct and not one of the four players to whom the New Zealand **WARNED**

Mike Brown
REPRIMANDED and fined £1,000 for staying out all night during tour and subsequently being **GUILTY**

Danny Care
NOT guilty of any misconduct. Did not drink excessively nor miss any team appointment. No **NOT GUILTY**

---

the judge. There had been no specific protocol about drinking or bringing back guests. Nor was there a curfew. In the light of all this, Blackett's response was 'The players should not be dropped for this error of judgment. All four players appear honest and truthful. I

> **ABOVE** Judge Blackett's report of 14 pages contained 7211 words. His judgment was to fine Ojo £500 and Brown £1000. Strettle and Care were cleared.

ABOVE A worried-looking Brian Ashton watches England's 33-10 win over Ireland in the 2008 Six Nations. It was to be his last Test in charge – a month later he was out of a job.

FACING PAGE The Bulls are celebrating, as well they should. Heyneke Meyer has just taken them to the Super 14 crown in 2007, the first time a South African side had won the title.

have seen or heard no evidence which has been tested to gainsay their denials.'

Brown was fined £1000 and reprimanded for staying out all night and being late for a physiotherapy appointment; Ojo received a fine of £500 and a reprimand for being a stop-out; Strettle, implicated in the 'kiss and tell', was warned to stay out of compromising situations; and Care was exonerated. Johnson's squad contains all four of the players named, with Danny Care in the elite unit and the other three in his Saxons line-up.

This is the end of the issue, but what about future discipline and patterns of behaviour by the players? Johnson earned a reputation for ruthlessness when he was a player, though he has no experience as a manager or a coach. Yet England chose him to superintend their team. When the Argentinian Marcelo Loffreda was unceremoniously booted out of Welford Road after barely seven months in charge, it might have been much better if the iconic Johnson had been appointed for a year or two as leader of the Tigers, for whom he played with such distinction.

Leicester have hardly hit the heights since they won the Heineken Cup in 2001. They were knocked out by Edinburgh at Murrayfield in this season's competition, and lost in the Premiership final to Wasps. They responded to Loffreda's departure by searching the world for a new coach and settled on Heyneke Meyer, who won four Currie Cups in five years with the Blue Bulls and led the Bulls to a Super 14 crown in 2007, the first time a South African side had won the title. It will be fascinating to see how well Meyer performs, as he attempts to return Leicester to their glory trail.

Leeds Carnegie had never been on a glory trail. Their lame season was all about avoiding relegation from the Premiership, which, as in 2002 and 2006, proved to be sadly inevitable. Throughout the season their director of rugby, Stuart Lancaster, was fond of telling anyone prepared to listen that the club's position in the top league would be maintained and he did not want to move elsewhere. Given the chance to move to Leicester, Wasps or Gloucester at twice the salary, you can bet your life he would have taken it. Money matters most.

Lancaster was recruited by the RFU Academy to join a growing band of coaches, and has been replaced at Leeds Carnegie by Neil Back and Andy Key. Rather than play any of their matches at West Park, which has been redeveloped at a cost of £6.5 million, Leeds have chosen to play at Headingley, where National One games are unlikely to attract attendances of more than 1500.

If Leeds Carnegie feel they have been unfortunate, the position at Kingston Park is hardly any better, where Newcastle have had another dire season struggling to keep their reputation intact. Their major sponsor, Northern Rock, has been in all sorts of trouble, and the club bade farewell to Mark Mayerhofler and the inspirational full back Matt Burke. The director of rugby, John Fletcher, was soon to follow, as were England internationals Toby Flood and Mathew Tait. What happens next is anyone's guess, though it will be no surprise if they are down among the also-rans in the coming season's Premiership.

Of wider concern is the shape of rugby in England, which is adopting the outline of football's Premiership. The template for this, and many other sports, is about Britons watching those from the rest of the world do well. The best are encouraged to come here, and with the Premiership in England among the top competitions in world rugby, we can provide the players with the rewards and facilities which can be financed by charging spectators premium prices, on a scale where they can be accommodated in relative luxury. The fact that the players are not qualified to play for England is of little interest to the clubs they join or, for that matter, themselves. Ask Arsenal. Football in England is not unlike a ten-month-long European championship. It is not about developing home-grown talent; it is about producing the most lucrative star-studded competition in the world.

Rugby union is following suit. The club game at the top of the tree has become a national activity for hosts. We are paying big money to watch the best players on the planet exhibit their skills on our doorstep. Were there a world championship for spectators, we would be at the top of the league.

To make life more interesting for the Premiership clubs, the RFU have struck an eight-year deal with them. Johnson will have the entire squad at his disposal for two weeks before the autumn internationals and for a similar period in advance of the Six Nations Championship. During a total of 14 weeks per season, the clubs expect to receive the sum of £146,250 per player by way of compensation. Much of this time the clubs will be participating in Premiership rugby, so their England-qualified players will be on leave. Why not invest the money and recruit some more overseas players who will not be involved? Why not indeed?

The abiding story of England's summer tour to New Zealand and the aftermath reminds me of Terence's dictum: *Jus summum sæpe summa est malitia*. The rigour of the law is often the hardest injustice.

This begs the question: was the law applied as rigorously as it could have been? If not, why not? Where was the injustice? What lessons have been learned? Will it happen again?

BELOW Thanks to Rob Andrew, Martin Johnson will have the entire England squad at his disposal for 14 weeks a season.

Geech Goes Back
the 2009 Lions Tour to South Africa

by MICK CLEARY

'The Lions will never be far from a player's thoughts during the 2009 Six Nations Championship.... This is the trip that he wants. This is the tour he wants to go on'

The detail is in place and eyes are being cast. The British & Irish Lions tour to South Africa next year is already taking shape. The outline may be faint, the playing squad yet to be finalised, but as head coach Ian McGeechan lies back and thinks of things to come, there will be a contented smile playing across his face. He knows what he wants.

He's already got what he wants in terms of his coaching team: shrewd men with the right instincts. They will play what is in front of them and that is all you can do as a Lions coach, never mind as a player. Pre-set ideas have little place on a Lions tour. The fallacy of that approach has been proved time and again, most recently in New Zealand in 2005. Fifty thousand supporters, meanwhile, who have already made tentative travel plans, will also be in good heart.

There may not have been a great return on the scoreboard from the respective tours last summer by the four Home Unions. A solitary Test victory (Scotland's over Argentina in a drawn series) from eight matches against the southern hemisphere is, on the face of it, no reason for cheer. However, the Lions trip is entirely different. The form guide at the moment is unreliable, the portents misleading. England may have been dubbed a 'great fraud' down in New Zealand during the summer, but the same would not be said of the Lions, not even by All Blacks fans who saw their side win at a canter against Sir Clive Woodward's side three years ago. The Lions have charisma, class and a chance. No one knows what sort of a chance because they do not exist yet as a real entity. No one knows who will come through with a surge during the upcoming Six Nations Championship, or who will feature as a part of brand-new combinations in the eyes of the Lions management.

The tour will be the focal point of the season for many players as they look to build momentum and impress selectors. It will be firmly etched into their plans as they fine-tune their conditioning programmes to make sure that there is enough left in the tank come June and July.

It was so evident from watching this year's tours to New Zealand, Australia, South Africa and Argentina that the players were, for the most part, pretty much a spent force. It's been a long haul from pre-World Cup training camps, through the tournament itself and on to Six Nations and European competitions. It's too much.

Is the Lions tour too much, then? Never mind two extra Tests at the end of an arduous haul through winter, the Lions schedule is ten matches, and that is shorter than usual. But as players returned home last June to wind down for a few weeks before hitting the pre-season training with a vengeance, the trip was there as a fixed entity with all its sporting and romantic overtones.

If you had taken a straw poll of every single Home Union player trudging down airplane steps on their arrival back in Britain and

FACING PAGE Ian McGeechan poses with mascot, having been appointed coach of the 2009 Lions tour to South Africa, scene of his triumph in 1997.

BELOW Bryan Habana streaks past Dan Carter during South Africa's 2008 Tri-Nations clash with the All Blacks at Wellington. The flying wing is one of the Springboks' most potent attacking weapons.

Ireland last June, not one of them would have baulked at the idea of embarking on the six-week trek round South Africa next year. It's an exciting prospect, primarily because it is unique.

What has McGeechan learned since taking office six months ago? He went on a fact-finding mission to South Africa in June accompanied by manager Gerald Davies. Their interest was first and foremost logistical, to get a feel for training venues and hotels. But they also wanted to sniff the air down in South Africa and gauge the strength and direction of Springbok rugby.

McGeechan did a similar thing in 1996, when he went under his own steam to see one of the great contests in world rugby – the All Blacks taking on the Boks in South Africa. New Zealand had never won a series there, an astounding fact when you consider how often teams play each other these days. McGeechan devised his winning strategy on that trip. Twelve months later, the Lions were victorious. This time he'll have seen the traditional Springbok virtues at work in their two-Test series victory over Wales: belligerent forward play and sharp, hard-running attacking from the likes of Jean de Villiers in the centre and Bryan Habana on the wing.

Wales were understrength, but McGeechan will have been pleased to see the way they rallied in the second Test, testament perhaps to the leadership qualities of Ryan Jones. Wing Shane Williams, bringing his tally to twelve tries in his last ten Tests, was as potent as ever, while Stephen Jones snatched back the fly-half mantle. Prop Gethin Jenkins also showed well.

FACING PAGE Wales's Grand Slam captain Ryan Jones in 2008 Six Nations action against Ireland in Dublin. Could he be the leader of the 2009 Lions?

BELOW John Bentley, one of the 1997 Lions' ex-rugby league contingent, crashes into Springbok Pieter Rossouw during the decisive second Test.

Ireland fared the best of all the Home Unions, giving a good account of themselves in both Wellington and Melbourne, really running the Wallabies close. Full back Rob Kearney looks a developing talent, and it was heartening to see lock Paul O'Connell step up to the mark. He too is a strong candidate for the Lions captaincy. Flanker David Wallace also shone under stress against the All Blacks. Scotland came back against Argentina but again relied heavily on Chris Paterson's boot. Ali Hogg was robust on the flank, while scrum half Mike Blair was sharp. As for England, flankers James Haskell and Tom Rees stood up to the test. Scrum half Danny Care was lively but has a long way to go yet.

So much for some early form indicators. McGeechan is too experienced, too canny, to write anybody out of contention at this stage. There are always bolters, players on the fringes, perhaps even overlooked by their national coaches, who will suddenly emerge and become irresistible in the eyes of the Lions selectors. In 1997 McGeechan read the prevailing mood of world rugby just right when he beefed up his squad with an influx of former rugby league players, or union guys with league experience, such as Alan Tait, Scott Gibbs, Allan Bateman, Scott Quinnell and John Bentley. Irishman Eric Miller made a significant charge through the ranks. Will Greenwood was uncapped by England but central to McGeechan's way of thinking.

What McGeechan wants to instil in his men over the next six months is the enduring appeal of the challenge. Here's what he said on the eve of departure to South Africa in 1997. The message is as true and forceful now as it was then.

'You simply cannot come to a Lions tour in a half-hearted frame of mind. You have to immerse yourself in the whole thing. You have to become part of the country you are travelling through. You have to accept the atmosphere you find there because you have helped to create it. It may be hostile, feverish, alien – but you are partly responsible for it, and you should accept it. The key is to come with an open mind, to accept the challenge and to embrace the experience.'

You can feel the hairs prickling on your neck just reading those words.

The Lions will never be far from a player's thoughts during the 2009 Six Nations Championship. Oh, he'll trot out the usual platitude of only taking one game at a time, and not getting too far ahead of himself. But deep down, the inner man won't be trying to delude himself. This is the trip that he wants. This is the tour he wants to go on. And all that despite the bad-vibes feel that has hung over the past two tours – to Australia in 2001 and to New Zealand four years later. The Lions missed a trick in 2001. They had a series victory within their grasp. A Jonny Wilkinson interception try, a dangerous tackle on Richard Hill that knocked him out of the running, a line-out steal by Justin Harrison on Martin Johnson – on such margins …

But there was a fractious atmosphere on that trip. It was not a happy time, although as Hill himself said, 'I wasn't there for a holiday. Of course, we had to work hard.'

Perhaps. There was a feeling, though, that head coach Graham Henry didn't get the best from his men. Four years later, the feeling was that Clive Woodward had too many men from which to get the best; that he couldn't see what was really needed.

There's no danger of McGeechan repeating those mistakes. One crack. That's all the Lions get at it. They congregate, they play, they break up – never to be a team together again. There is no time to perfect systems, to hone defensive alignments or fine-tune line-out sequences in the manner that every international team now does.

Players are under stress. Time is short. The challenge is immense. But that's why we all keep coming back for more. As for Lions selection, it's ever fluid, ever fascinating. It will be no different this time around.

BELOW Another contender for the Lions captaincy, Paul O'Connell puts his body in the way of a Neemiah Tialata charge during last June's Test against the All Blacks at Wellington.

Golden Centenary
100 Years of Wallaby Touring

by CHRIS THAU

'The back division of Phillip Carmichael, Russell, John Hickey, Bede Smith and Daniel Carroll remained unchanged and performed superbly on the day'

THE AUSTRALIAN RUGBY FOOTBALL TEAM (THE WALLABIES).

(1) D. B. Carroll (2) P. Carmichael (3) C. E. Parkinson (4) W. Dix (5) M. McArthur (6) H. F. Daly (7) F. Wood (vice-capt). (8) J. Hickey (9) J. M. Stevenson (10) Ward Prentice (11) T. S. Griffin (12) J. T. Barnett (13) E. F. Mandible (14) J. McMahon (Manager) (15) H. M. Moran (capt.) (16) F. Bede Smith (17) C. Russell (18) C. H. McKivat (19) A. J. McCabe (20) B. R. Craig (21) T. J. Richards (22) P. Flanagan (23) P. McCue (24) S. A. Middleton (25) P. H. Burge (26) N. E. Row (27) C. A. Hammond (28) C. McMurtrie (29) E. J. McIntyre (30) S. M. Wickham.

I t is 100 years since the day – 19 September 1908 – when RMS *Omrah* landed at Plymouth at the beginning of what history recorded as the first ever Australian rugby tour of the British Isles. The Australians were the third side to arrive from the Dominions in the 20th century after the 1905 New Zealanders and the 1906 South Africans, and the tour was eagerly anticipated, since reports about the prowess of the Australians had already filtered back home from A. F Harding's Anglo-Welsh Lions, still in Sydney at the time of the Wallabies' departure.

ABOVE The 1908 Wallabies touring party to the British Isles and North America. Tour skipper 'Paddy' Moran is fifth from left in the middle row.

Besides being the first visit of the Australians to Britain, the 1908 tour made history in other ways. It was the first time Australia's rugby representatives, though wearing the New South Wales Waratah on their jerseys, went by the nickname of 'Wallabies'. While Australia had played Test rugby before, it was the first time they had taken on England or Wales. The team also performed a war cry, described by the team management as the 'Natives Greetings to Strangers in Peace'.

An equally historically significant first occurred with the ninth match of the UK leg of the tour (two warm-up matches had been played in Australia), in which the Wallabies defeated English county champions Cornwall to win the gold medal for rugby at the 1908 London Olympic Games. Australia had already defeated Cornwall 18-5 in the tour's third match in Camborne but arrived in London having suffered the first defeat (3-8) of the trip at the hands of Llanelli, in circumstances described by Tom Richards, one of the leading Australian forwards: 'On arriving at the playing field there was a saucepan on top of each goalpost, and a mighty crowd, delirious with expectancy, singing and working up enthusiasm to a great pitch, filling the heads and hearts of their players with a primitive impulse to tear in and fight with deadly earnest, showing no quarter, giving no respite.'

On Saturday 24 October, the Wallabies took on a powerful London side, who were expected to emulate the example of Llanelli and put the visitors to the sword. But the Wallabies, led by a gallant Herbert 'Paddy' Moran, begged to differ. An interception try by Charles Russell was the only score of the match, with Moran leading his men by example, with his left arm strapped to his body, having dislocated his shoulder in the first half.

The organisers of the Olympic rugby tournament, which included RFU honorary secretary and former president G. Rowland Hill, expected a minimum of three teams to take part, but France, due to play Cornwall in the opening match, withdrew at the last moment. There being no representation from any other rugby-playing nation, the one and only match of the tournament was between the Wallabies and Cornwall, representing Great Britain. Some sources suggest that the Welsh union had declined to take part, though it is unlikely to have been invited, since Wales was part and parcel of Great Britain, who could enter only one team.

Whereas in the earlier match against the visitors Cornwall could not field their best team, on Monday 26 October 1908, the day of the Olympic final, Cornwall were probably at full strength, including in their ranks no less than five current or later England internationals – John Jackett, Bert Solomon, Tommy Wedge, James Davey and Arthur Wilson. The Wallabies had made few changes from the team that played the previous Saturday. With both skipper Moran and vice-captain Fred Wood out of action, the side was captained by scrum half Chris McKivat with Arthur McCabe at outside half. The back division of Phillip Carmichael, Russell, John Hickey, Bede Smith and Daniel Carroll remained unchanged and performed superbly on the day, serviced impeccably by an inspired McKivat playing behind a dynamic pack who hardly put a foot wrong, with Richards and

Syd Middleton mentioned in despatches. 'All the men behind the scrummage in the winning team played so well that it would be unfair to mention anyone for special praise,' wrote Philip Trevor in *The Daily Telegraph*. The Wallabies scored seven tries on a wet and greasy pitch at Shepherd's Bush to win 32-3, their second biggest margin of the UK leg of the tour. Their top scorer was full back Carmichael, with four conversions and one penalty goal, followed by Carroll, McCabe and Hickey with two tries each and Richards with one.

There has been a fair amount of debate about the medals awarded to the winning team. According to some reports, all members of the Australian team received a certificate and a 'handsome silver medal' at the end of the Olympic final. It was also claimed that the 15 players who took part in the match were subsequently presented with a 'suitably inscribed gold medal'. There is a mention of a 10-guinea gold medal presented to the team as a whole. Several of the 1908 Olympic certificates still exist and adorn

the walls of various clubs and unions in Australia. However, only one gold medal seems to have survived, in the vaults of one of the Sydney banks, suggesting that perhaps the accounts mentioning medals for all team members were incorrect. This version of the events is supported by the story of the runners-up, Cornwall, who, although they received certificates for all their players, were presented with a single silver medal, which the team decided to allow one of the players to keep for good.

With the planned match against France cancelled due to poor weather, the Wallabies left for the United States after their thirtieth match of the UK tour, a defeat of Plymouth by 15-6. Besides the 30 games played in the UK, the Australians played four in Australia (the two before departure as well as two on their return) plus four in the USA and Canada. Overall they won 32 of these 38 matches, drew one and lost five, including an epic Test against Wales in December 1908 in which the Wallabies' were defeated 9-6.

Paradoxically, the purely amateur 1908 team contributed to a temporary crisis in rugby union in Australia, as the following year about half of the tourists 'defected' to the professional code, the players having been the object of a vigorous campaign by rugby league entrepreneurs keen to capitalise on their 'market value'. It has been argued that the defection to league would have been reduced had skipper Herbert Moran returned with the team to Australia at the conclusion of the tour, rather than staying in the UK to pursue his medical studies, since many of the undecided players might have followed his advice rather than that of the group of league intermediaries within the team.

INTERNATIONAL SCENE

Robbie Deans
Teambuilding Beyond the Tasman

by RAECHELLE INMAN

'Australian rugby fans are hoping that this is the start of the Wallabies returning to an expansive and exciting "Deans brand" of rugby'

'Dingo Deans', 'Aussie Robbie' – call him what you will, but New Zealander Robbie Deans is being hailed as the saviour of Australian rugby. Australian Rugby Union CEO John O'Neill said he had every confidence Australia can move into a new golden era with Deans at the helm. 'We don't hide from the fact we need to improve our win-loss ratio and produce a style of rugby our fans will embrace on a consistent basis,' O'Neill said.

With the appointment of Deans, a foreigner, as Wallaby coach until the end of 2011, the Australian rugby community is hoping O'Neill will be able to emulate the success he achieved as CEO of Soccer Australia. In that role he signed Dutch coach Guus Hiddink, who masterminded the Socceroos' 2006 World Cup fairy tale.

It's an interesting twist of fate that Deans almost didn't make the move across the Tasman. Indeed, it was a fortunate turn of events for Australian rugby that the New Zealand Rugby Union failed to present Deans with the opportunity he really coveted – the role as head coach of the All

Blacks. The Australians showed how much they valued the 48-year-old Crusaders coach by allowing him to make a late application for the Wallabies job, after his All Black ambitions were thwarted. Deans duly became the first foreigner to coach the Australian national rugby union team, beating five Aussies for the position: David Nucifora of the Auckland Blues; NSW Waratahs coach Ewen McKenzie; broadcaster and former Wallabies coach Alan Jones; Laurie Fisher of the ACT Brumbies; and John Muggleton, who was the Wallabies assistant coach.

Deans says that he was delighted that the opportunity was still there, 'because there was a genuine risk that it could have really lapsed'.

'It's great to be somewhere you're wanted.'

Despite the similarities between Australia and New Zealand, a bitter rivalry exists between the two nations when it comes to rugby, and a few vocal members of the Australian rugby community weren't so welcoming. Journalist and former Wallaby Peter FitzSimons said on New Zealand radio, 'It's a sad day for Australian rugby when we get a Kiwi coach.' The reality is that Deans's appointment is a fact of professional sporting life.

Just as Australia's Eddie Jones contributed to South Africa's 2007 World Cup success, Deans offers a unique insight into New Zealand rugby, having coached the Crusaders, who make up half the All Black team. Bledisloe Cup matches are always fiercely contested and it will be a tremendous advantage for the Wallabies to have someone with intimate knowledge of All Blacks strategy and player intelligence in their camp. The heightened level of meaning for these clashes, where Deans will go head to head with Graham Henry, brings with it a new degree of intensity and passion.

The prospect of the Wallabies being more competitive in Bledisloe Cup contests and building a side that is capable of victory in the World Cup in New Zealand in 2011 has most in Australian rugby circles excited and optimistic about Deans's selection. Former Wallaby captain John Eales singles out Deans's composure and how that is reflected in the teams he has coached. 'The Crusaders did have the best defence in the Super 14, but they also had the best attack. To get one of those working is good, so to have both is a real highlight of his talent,' Eales commented.

His coaching record speaks for itself. After taking over as Crusaders head coach in 2000, Deans guided the New Zealand side to a record five Super Rugby crowns, capturing the title in his first season and again in 2002, 2005, 2006 and 2008. From 2001 to 2003, Deans was All Black assistant coach to John Mitchell. During this period New Zealand won twenty-two, drew one and lost four of the Tests they played; this included winning the Tri-Nations twice and recovering the Bledisloe Cup in 2003 after a five-year absence.

So, how does he achieve this level of success? Rather than focusing on winning a particular game or series, Deans talks more about the processes involved, the concept of 'the group' and collective understandings and deriving enjoyment. It seems in the Deans method that every

LEFT Coach Deans takes charge of Wallabies training ahead of the June 2008 Test against Ireland. According to ARU chairman Peter McGrath, 'In terms of our playing ranks, we are on the doorstep of generational change. We believe Robbie Deans is the man to move us into that new era.'

player in the team needs to take ownership of their own actions and needs to be aware of the contribution they are offering. If these foundations are strong, the results and successes are a natural outcome. 'Things I derive satisfaction from are helping individuals to progress ... but also helping a team to gather and then effectively combine to harness the skill set that they bring, such that hopefully we enjoy our time together.'

Deans doesn't try to emulate anyone else's style of coaching because 'if you try to be someone else it is difficult to be spontaneous'. He talks about having acquired knowledge through his experiences. 'I am lucky to have had around me some people who have been pretty influential. From a playing end, guys like Alex Wyllie and Doug Bruce among others ... Alex was one bloke who had a big impact on our playing group and a lot of that group went on to give back to the game and coach, so obviously it was a positive experience.

'One of the motivating factors is to offer my playing group ... an experience that they enjoy, like I was lucky enough to have.'

Deans builds on this, revealing a little more about his depth of thought. 'We are essentially the same people – as I was told once – apart from the people we meet and the books that we read ... one of my early books that I remember, because it was probably the first book I used in a coaching context, was Pat Riley's *The Winner Within*. That was when I first latched onto the fact that there are other people out there who have been through what we are going through and they are a good source of ideas.

'The one thing that is a bit scary is the more that I learn the more I realise that I need to learn. You enter with a certain amount of knowledge and you think it's significant but then you realise how little you do know and that's just the nature of the industry. It's such a dynamic and challenging industry you've got to keep seeking and seeking to extend yourself before your own people.'

Deans feels that open, honest and strong communication is preferable, if that is something that the group sees as a priority. He says, 'The key is that everyone has access and the opportunity to contribute and have a sense of involvement and belonging.'

On arrival in Australia, one of Deans's first initiatives to improve the Wallaby players' communication skills was to put players into different groups for training drills, mixing up forwards and backs and ensuring players from each state mingled. This marked the start of his creation of an authentic community. Deans routinely talks with his players and creates a safe environment in which everyone can contribute. To the suggestion that a lot of coaches don't ask players for their opinions, he quips, 'So how do they know? Awareness is everything.

'It's around your routines and processes, how you live day to day and what opportunity there is for people to have input and access and a sense of contribution and involvement. You can say we are going to have open and honest communication but if your routine or processes don't reinforce that you won't end up there.

'It's only as good as what people bring to it ultimately ... but you generally end up where you aim or close to it.'

One of his biggest advantages is taking on a Wallaby side with no baggage or allegiances, which has created a level playing field. 'I come in with no preconceived ideas. I'm not too concerned with what has happened in the past.

'The exciting and interesting thing is where will we be? There are no guarantees for players. There are going to be opportunities and who knows?'

A recent criticism of the Wallabies has been that ego has been allowed to get in the way and impacted on their performance. 'Belief is valuable as long as it's not misdirected, misguided or misused,' Deans said. 'In this industry you've got to keep things pretty real otherwise you'll be "earthed" pretty quickly, so sooner or later someone will impart the understanding,' he continued with a smile.

The Crusaders clearly developed a trademark 'real' approach under Deans. You only had to spend an hour or two at training or talking with the players and the friendships and enjoyment that the players share were obvious. At the pinnacle of his time with Canterbury, Andrew Mehrtens summed it up, 'We do a lot of hard work together but there is a real equality in the team. No matter how much rugby experience or what you've achieved you are on the same level as any other guy ... the culture of taking the "mickey" out of each other really helps, so that guys don't get too big for their boots.'

Under Deans the Crusaders played as a team that was greater than the sum of its individuals. There was an absence of selfish play and the amount of support and back-up the players gave each other was undeniable. Deans will have an opportunity to develop a new ethos with the Australian team. 'If you've got an underlying caring it's amazing what you can do. If you don't have that then quite often that sort of interaction can become destructive.'

Deans needs players around him who display a level of emotional intelligence that means they are genuinely open to learn and stretch themselves. 'Everyone's in a different space, I would suggest it is a defining factor in terms of having longevity at the top end, you don't "park up" and have longevity because there's a queue of people who want what you've got and they will be prepared to seek improvement. It's stimulating and it makes it more fun!'

Many try to unravel how Deans is able to create a unique and sustainable culture that underpins success. 'Culture to me is what is there when, as a dedicated leader, I'm not,' Deans explained. 'It's the combination of a lot of little things ... a lot of effort, nothing happens without effort. That effort is owned by the individuals who are part of that group.

'I'm a great believer that the invisible factors are often the points of difference. The stuff you can't see, but you can feel. When you're on the other side of the chalk with a team, they send you a message. You see it. You feel it. You have a sense of how long they are going to persevere, and what it means to them. The more we can create that in terms of meaning to us, and strengthen the bonds, then as it gets difficult, that's when those things will kick in. And it will be that which will be the point of difference.'

He describes top-level rugby as an emotional industry. 'It's not like nine-to-five, you've got to give a piece of yourself in this industry because you've got to face yourself.

'Essentially every time you strap on your boots and run out there you are in some way or form challenging yourself by having others challenge you as well, so that involves emotion, you can't get away from that.'

While he looks at both performance and potential when selecting his players, he sees attitude and motivation as critical elements. 'Character is a big one for me. You have to look at the character of your people and the reason for that is that not everyone's needs are met so how people respond under that circumstance is important because that can impact on the people around them.

'Those that clearly enjoy what they do are generally preferable to have in the group because if they don't enjoy what they do they are quite demanding in terms of energy and they can be demanding on the people around them.'

One of the major issues in Australian rugby in the professional years has been a perceived lack of depth. Deans doesn't have the luxury of being wasteful with talent as there simply aren't the numbers in the player pool. But rather than focusing on weaknesses, Deans looks at the opportunities. 'I see a lot of potential, I see a lot of scope, I see a group that's intelligent and really committed and enjoy what they do and those are the three key components.'

From the outset Deans has always admired the characteristic Australian strength and 'never-say-die' attitude. 'My playing experience and my coaching experience has reinforced for me the toughness of Australians. It is certainly a trait I would like to see go forward, because in this industry, it is never plain sailing. The moment you are in calm waters, you're probably at risk. You're not going anywhere. So that's a quality Australians have, probably because it's a bigger market and it's tougher to make it.'

After Deans's first training session as coach, Wallabies lock Nathan Sharpe commented that 'one of the most pleasing things for all the guys is that he wants us to play what's in front of us.'

'So rather than being really structured and, I guess, oriented to playing predetermined phases, he wants guys in the right position, to make decisions and then back yourself. And that's a good thing for all the guys to know, because if the coach backs you to make the right decisions, then 90 per cent of the time hopefully you will.'

Deans says, 'Every side is second-guessing themselves; every side goes into a game with some preconceived ideas about what they think may be effective on the day but the fact that we're second-guessing each other means that if that's not the case, if that's not what you're confronted with, in the moment then you've got to have the ability to adapt.'

It has been refreshing to see a strong emphasis on using the ball, and Australian rugby fans are hoping that this is the start of the Wallabies returning to an expansive and exciting 'Deans brand' of rugby.

To help players find a healthy work/life balance, Deans ensures that windows of opportunity are available in the playing and training programme and

LEFT A member of an All Black dynasty, Deans played five Tests. His younger brother Bruce played ten, while great uncle Bob scored the disallowed try against Wales in what turned out to be the only defeat of the 1905 'Original' All Blacks on their tour of Britain.

FACING PAGE Deans with Ali Williams after the Crusaders' 2008 Super 14 final win over the Waratahs in Christchurch, the coach's last match in charge.

encourages them to get away, chase an interest or hobby or spend time with family and friends. 'You've got to learn the art of switching on and off. You can't stay mentally up all the time. This is something the players have to learn as well. If you don't get that balance, you will go into decline over time.'

Deans says his own time away from the game is essential, especially family time. He is a qualified teacher and his wife, Penny, is a qualified French teacher. They met in the varsity library in Canterbury. They have been married for 21 years and have three children – son Sam and daughters Annabelle and Sophie. 'They're a great source of perspective.'

Robbie Deans started out in the Canterbury representative rugby team in 1979 as a first five-eighth. But the arrival of Wayne Smith soon saw him switch to full back. Deans first achieved national honours as a player in 1983, when Wellington's Allan Hewson was unavailable for the tour of Scotland and England. He played both internationals on that tour, and then in 1984 on the tour of Australia ousted Hewson to gain his final three caps in the Bledisloe Cup series. A serious knee injury later that season, though, ended his All Black Test career. In his five Test appearances, Deans scored 50 points, and his goal-kicking was a key factor in New Zealand's victories in the second and third Tests against the Wallabies in 1984. At provincial level, Deans ended his Canterbury playing career with an impressive 1641 points from 146 appearances, before returning in a coaching and management capacity in 1997, eventually taking over as head coach of the Crusaders and winning all those titles. He is proud of what he accomplished as a coach at Canterbury. 'That's been hugely satisfying, good to be able to walk away in the way that I did.'

So with the overwhelming pressure and expectation of his new-found nation, does it feel weird to be a Kiwi coaching the Wallabies? 'No. It feels natural, because it's just more of the same because I'm coaching, and when you're coaching you're dealing with people and the game and as a coach your job is to facilitate performance and that's what we do.

'I will concede that the only moment that has really felt novel was the first team talk but that was more of my sensitivity around the fact that I was talking to a Wallaby team and I just had an empathy or an awareness that I couldn't be sure what was going through their minds under that circumstance.

'Now I've got that behind me … I don't think I'll have that moment again.'

It seems the prayers of the Australian rugby faithful have been answered.

Forging Ahead
A Revolution in German Rugby
by CHRIS THAU

'German rugby is turning a corner after many years of silent and efficient development. Its growing potential is confirmed by the emergence of several high-quality ... players'

Germany is probably the oldest rugby country on the Continent, since the game developed a strong presence there under the influence of the English public schools. A number of English schools opened in Switzerland and Germany during the mid-19th century, with Germany having several well-regarded establishments, in Heidelberg-Neuenheim, Frankfurt, Stuttgart, Dresden, Bremen and Hanover. The curriculum of the English public schools in Germany was fairly similar to that of their counterparts in England. Consequently the schoolboys, both British and German, played both football codes, Association and Rugby. William Cail, the twelfth RFU president, attended the school in Stuttgart, while the founding fathers of German rugby, Ferdinand Wilhelm Fricke and Professor Edward Hill Ullrich, learned the game in Hanover and Heidelberg respectively.

As the number of players grew, several rugby clubs got started in Heidelberg, Frankfurt and Hanover, the first of which, Heidelberger Ruderklub (Rowing Club), celebrated its centenary in 1972. By the turn of the 20th century, enough clubs were operational to require the formation of a governing body – hence the establishment of Deutscher Rugby Verband (DRV) in 1900, the oldest Continental union. One of the early decisions of the newly formed organisation was to sanction the participation of one of its clubs, Frankfurt 1880 FC, in the 1900 Olympics in Paris, where the German players impressed with their rugby know-how and sporting demeanour. Frankfurt FC, who had visited London a few times during the 1880s, developed strong bonds with both the Harlequins and Blackheath clubs, the latter giving them a set of jerseys and the right to use the black-and-red strip in perpetuity.

By 1927 Germany were strong enough to defeat France (17-16), at the time a Five Nations regular. As France's relationship with the four Home Unions soured following allegations of violence and overt professionalism, at the end of the 1930-31 season the Home Unions broke off relations with French rugby 'due to the unsatisfactory condition of the Game of Rugby Football as managed and played in France'. The isolation of France was the gain of the Continental unions, who at the instigation of the French and German federations formed the Fédération Internationale de Rugby Amateur (FIRA) in 1934.

German, Romanian and Italian rugby benefited most from the French exile. Germany – already a power to be reckoned with after their unexpected yet thoroughly deserved 1927 win over France – became a genuine force by the late 1930s, managing to beat France again in 1938. However, after the war, German rugby somehow failed to recapture its former glory and status. Split in two by the division of the country into East and West Germany and confronted with the upsurge of professional games in the West and the obsession with Olympic medals in the East, rugby declined into oblivion. West Germany's last act of defiance was to defeat the up-and-coming Romania in Bucharest in 1972, while in East Germany rugby was kept alive just because it was played in the West.

This season, coached by the duo Rudolf Finsterer and Mark Kuhlmann, Germany have returned to the first division of the Continental competition, the European Nations Cup, after an absence of five years. The German team, captained by dynamic lock forward Jens Schmidt, also reached the final stages of round three of the RWC 2007 European zone qualifiers, in which they narrowly lost to Spain in a home-and-away tie. Although they failed to reach round four, the matches in RWC 2007

provided an opportunity for an intensive campaign of promotion and sponsorship, which paid dividends as over 8000 spectators attended the country's match against the Netherlands in Hanover. The success of the German team and the thrilling performances of players of the likes of Robert Mohr, Sacha Fischer, Colin Grzanna, Tim Coly, Clemens von Grumbkow, Kieron Davies and captain Schmidt inspired the thousands of children watching the matches from the stands of the stadia in Hanover and Heidelberg.

German rugby is turning a corner after many years of silent and efficient development. Its growing potential is confirmed by the emergence of several high-quality professional players who ply their trade in the highly competitive French game, of whom 7ft lock forward Sacha Fischer, whose career in French rugby included stints with Bourgoin, Bordeaux and Perigueux, and No. 8 Robert Mohr, the captain of La Rochelle, are the best known.

It is former Romanian international Peter Ianusevici, an ethnic German, who is regarded as the author of the 'German rugby revolution'. He was recruited by the

ABOVE AND RIGHT Echoes from the past. A photograph of the Frankfurt 1880 team that represented Germany at the 1900 Olympics in Paris, and a Frankfurt 1880 club cap.

ABOVE Robert Mohr, Germany's No. 8 and captain of French professional second division club La Rochelle, out and about in his home town of Hanover.

German union as national coach in 1993, but after several years at the helm he took over the technical department at DRV. Among his players when he was in charge of the German national team were several members of the Himmer rugby dynasty, of which Volker is the current DRV secretary.

'It is difficult to quantify Peter's contribution to the recent development of German rugby,' says Himmer. 'Peter coached the national team for several years and while setting up standards for the elite game, he has worked hard to expand the grass-root programme, mainly in schools, by launching regular rugby courses with PE students of leading German universities, with the PE teachers in schools, as well as leading refresher programmes with coaches, as well as helping to set up regional Rugby Academies, which already operate in five states.'

According to Ianusevici, whose coaching pedigree is as comprehensive as his playing career, it is numbers, tradition and athletic quality that form the framework of development. The DRV technical director had a distinguished career in rugby development in Romania before taking over the Romanian national team before RWC 1991. He coached Romania to an 18-12 win over Scotland in Bucharest in August 1991, then to their best RWC performance to date, although he still regards the years spent in development as the most fulfilling part of his career.

'For a long time German rugby was like a pyramid upside down. That means we had more senior players than juniors, which is definitely counterproductive for both development and elite selection. We managed to change that, but we still need to increase the numbers of youngsters coming into the game,' Ianusevici said.

'We have promoted the game in our main strongholds in the North, South and Central regions, through traditional methods, that is promoting through our clubs, promotional events and through family, which in Germany is a very powerful tool for recruitment. To give you an example, Robert Mohr, who captains a professional club in the French league, is the third generation rugby player, not to mention the Himmers, Schmidt etc. In order to help the game expand in schools, we went into universities and set up rugby courses for PE students, so when they graduated, they had rugby as an option in their career. This led to a huge increase in numbers as we expanded our school system in five German states.

'Naturally, as the numbers increased, the athleticism of the players joining the game has improved, not to mention the size and levels of skill. Unlike other unions we are mindful about recruiting too many overseas players, who are eligible to play through their family lineage, because it could be counterproductive. We must try to maintain a balance between the infusion of overseas talent and locally grown players. The overseas option is important but it is short term. We must make rugby more popular in Germany, must convince parents that rugby is not a violent game, that children enjoy the physical edge and that they could eventually make a living as professionals. Still a lot to do, but Germany has proved that in the right environment, with the right players they can do it,' Ianusevici concluded.

BELOW Clemens von Grumbkow in action for Germany against Georgia in the European Sevens at Hanover in July 2008. Like Robert Mohr, the centre is one of several German players plying their trade in France – in von Grumbkow's case with RC Orléans in Federal League Division One.

Passion and Talent
Looking to the Future in the Pacific
by RAECHELLE INMAN

'If a player represents another nation at open level in fifteen- or seven-man rugby, even once, this prohibits him from returning to play for his home nation'

The Pacific Islands are well known for having two of the essential ingredients needed to achieve great success in international rugby: passion and talent. Rugby is unequivocally the number one sport in Fiji, Tonga and Samoa, and the people genuinely love it. A testament to their abundance of natural athleticism and ability is the significant number of Pacific Islanders, and those of Pacific Island heritage, currently playing outside of the Islands in top-level rugby competitions in Europe, Japan, New Zealand, Australia – and even in rugby league.

Many of these players represent other nations. Among those currently playing at the highest level for the All Blacks are Keven Mealamu, Rodney So'oialo, Jerome Kaino, John Schwalger, Sione Lauaki and Sitiveni Sivivatu, while the current Wallaby squad includes Lote Tuqiri, George Smith, Digby Ioane, Wycliff Palu and Tatafu Polota-Nau. If all the best players of Pacific Island origin played for their national team on a consistent basis, these sides would be extremely competitive. However, there is no incentive for these players to represent their country, except for national pride. The reality is that players have to earn an income and sentimentality doesn't pay the bills.

And it's not just those who have been 'poached' by other nations that are the issue. A considerable number of players are involved in top-class provincial or club competitions such as the Super 14 or Heineken Cup as well as the many Islanders playing for wealthy clubs in Japan. In some cases, these players don't risk injury to play for their national side; in others, their clubs simply don't release them.

More of a level playing field exists in Sevens. The players from Fiji, Samoa and Tonga who play in the IRB Sevens World Series competition are generally all locals, living and playing their rugby in the Islands. The Tier One unions likewise generally field teams in these tournaments without their professional international and provincial players. So the sides are more evenly matched.

And the Pacific Island nations are very competitive when it comes to Sevens. In the last IRB series, Samoa and Fiji finished third and fourth respectively behind New Zealand and South Africa. And Tonga were only slotted in to compete in three out of the eight tournaments, but they finished in the competition table ahead of France and Canada, who each competed in all eight events, and only a handful of points behind Scotland, Wales and Australia, who also contested the full series.

Watching the Island teams playing in the seven-a-side competitions is entertaining because of their flair as playmakers and finishers, while to glimpse their potential in the 15-man game, one only has to look at the performances of Fiji and Tonga in the 2007 Rugby World Cup. Fiji defeated Wales and played an unbelievable game in the quarter-finals against South Africa, the eventual winners. And Tonga went within five points of causing the biggest upset of the event when they were defeated just 30-25 by South Africa in their pool match.

Yet despite their raw enthusiasm and natural aptitude for the game, the Pacific Island teams have only sporadically challenged the Tier One nations on the world rugby stage in the 15-a-side game.

ABOVE Graham Dewes scores Fiji's winning try in their 38-34 win over Wales at RWC 2007.

FACING PAGE Tonga-born Sione Lauaki playing for the Pacific Islanders against South Africa in 2004. He made his debut for the All Blacks against Fiji the following year.

The Islands face a number of challenges as they strive in their quest to be competitive more consistently. As part of a broad range of initiatives to support the growth and profile in the region, the concept of playing a combined Pacific Island team emerged in 2002. This enterprise was the result of a combined decision between the Fijian, Tongan and Samoan unions and was approved by the council of the International Rugby Board (IRB). The combined Pacific Islanders team was added to the international matches and tour fixtures schedule.

In 2004 the team played Test matches against Australia, New Zealand and South Africa. They were defeated in all three Tests but competed extremely well – the biggest losing margin was 15 points. Two years later, they toured the UK, playing Wales, Scotland and Ireland. Once again, they were defeated in each of the Tests, by respectable margins against Wales (20-38) and Scotland (22-34), although they conceded a bigger losing margin in their clash with Ireland, going down by 61 points to 17. It should be noted that warm-up games were not possible on the 2006 tour, since selected players would not have been released for matches outside the international Test window, which covers a period of three weeks. In 2008 the Pacific Islanders are scheduled to take on England, France and Italy.

The head coach of both the Fijian national team and the combined side, Ilivasi Tabua, sees the Pacific Islanders concept as having some short-term monetary, development and exposure benefits but not as the long-term solution. 'I don't see it as the future of Pacific Island rugby; you have the same concept with the British Lions,' Tabua said. 'They still have their own identity but it's another way for them to voice their identity, this time as the Pacific Islands as a whole,' he added.

Tabua, along with his two assistant coaches, Quddus Fielea (the current Tonga national coach) and Niko Palamo (Samoa's national coach), will select the squad based on merit, rather than a quota system from across the three nations.

'This is a performance tour, not a development tour,' Tabua explained. 'We pick the best team available because we want to be seen [as competitive] in Europe.

'This tour is another avenue to raise our concern about giving us an even playing field and the opportunity to have the privilege to play against Tier One countries.'

Selection for the 2008 tour is based on how players performed in the 2007 Rugby World Cup and the recent Pacific Nations Cup, in which Fiji, Tonga and Samoa had the chance to test their skills against Japan, New Zealand Maori and Australia A.

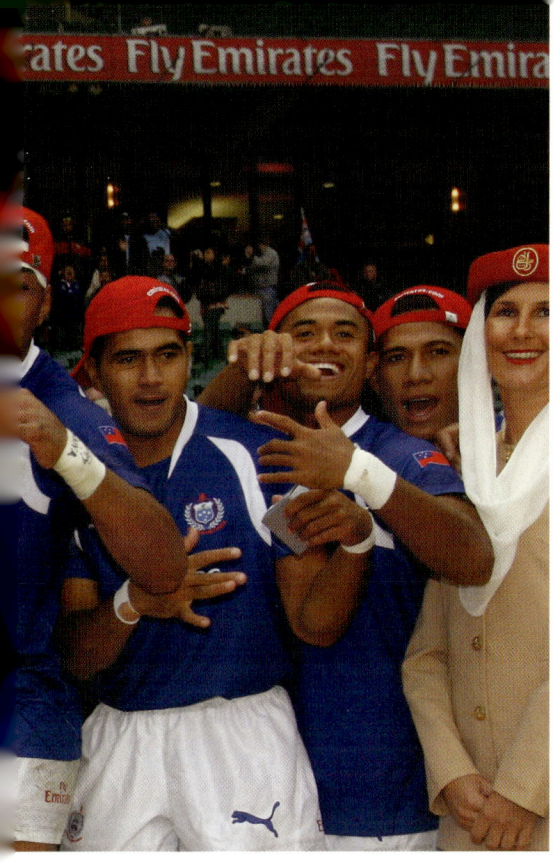

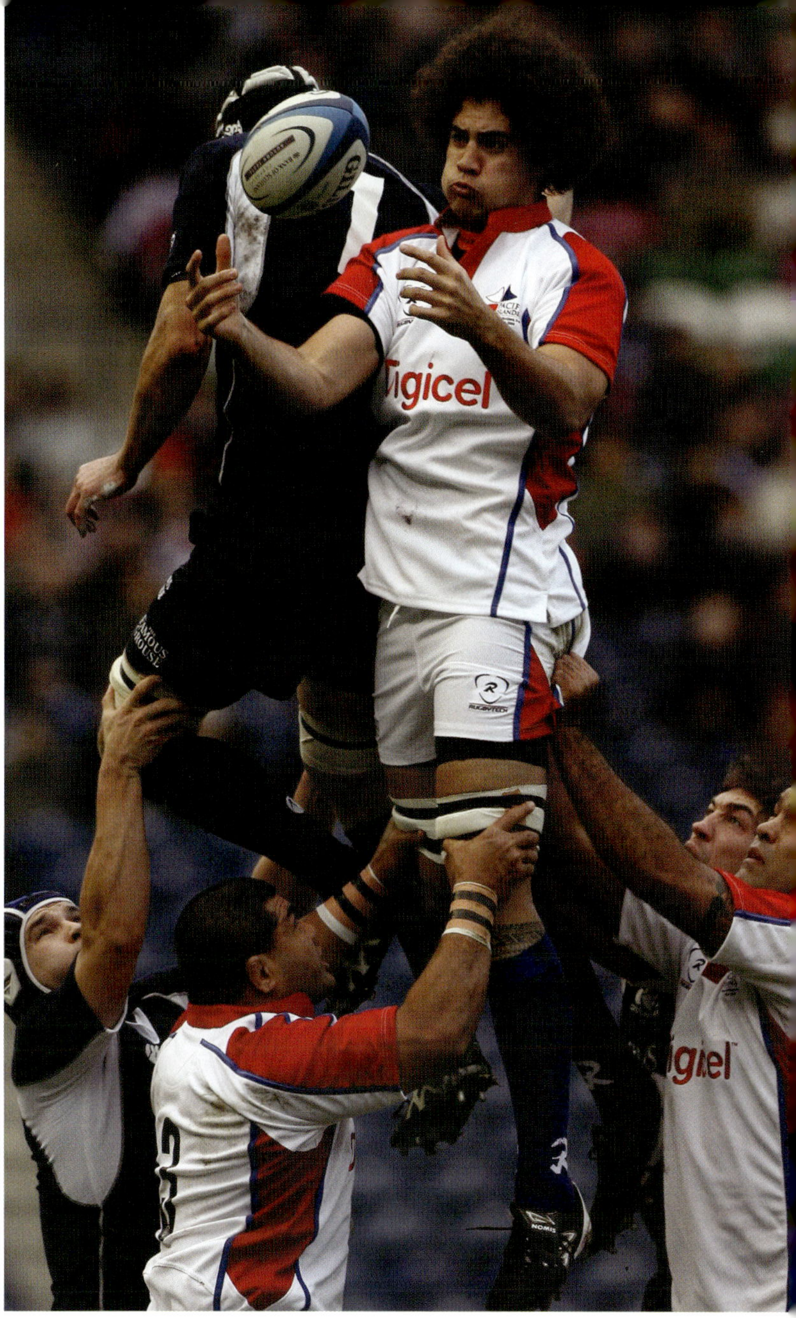

ABOVE Island teams enjoy success in international Sevens, where sides tend to be more evenly matched. This year the Samoans won the IRB England Sevens at Twickenham, beating Fiji 19-14 in the final.

RIGHT Dan Leo snaffles line-out ball for the Pacific Islanders against Scotland in 2006. New Zealand-born, Leo plays international rugby for Samoa.

Tabua has high expectations of the northern hemisphere visit. 'You don't go into any competitions not thinking you can win the games, or you might as well not go into the competition,' he said. 'If we win two out of three it would be good, or even three out of three, but every game is going to be tough.'

Tonga coach Fielea also is optimistic about the tour because of the upside for the individual players, who will have a brilliant opportunity to share best practice and develop their skills.

'I think it helps in that this year we don't have any other international matches playing as Tonga ... because we are out of the IRB tour match window ... so this is our only chance for us to expose some of our younger players that will take us to the 2011 World Cup,' Fielea said.

However, Fielea would prefer it if he had the opportunity for the Tongan side to play a series of Test matches, with his best players available. He clearly believes that playing as a combined team 'doesn't really help each individual country'.

The Islands are very keen to improve their position in the world rankings, but they are faced with a dilemma and it is extremely frustrating as history continues to repeat itself. Money is the key problem. Two potential, but highly unlikely, solutions are: the Islands are blessed with a sudden surge of ongoing sponsorship dollars; or they miraculously find a generous benefactor. This lack of funding means that players have been forced to chase lucrative contracts offshore, particularly in

Europe. This leaves their home nations hamstrung, apart from at World Cup time, because their best are not available during the southern hemisphere season.

How does Bob Tuckey, a member of the Pacific Island Tour Organising Committee and a former vice-chairman of the IRB with a Pacific Islands portfolio, see the future of Pacific Island rugby? 'A brilliant one, but it really all depends upon the SANZAR organisation in the first instance and also the IRB to some degree. Unless teams from all three unions are competing in the SANZAR competitions in their own right then the future will mimic the present,' Tuckey commented. 'If SANZAR brings them in then, for the first time since professionalism, they will be able to reach their full potential,' he added.

Early in 2007, at a meeting of Pacific Rugby Limited, a strategic vision and high-level goals for Pacific Islanders rugby were agreed. The vision is for self-sufficiency and inclusion within commercially viable professional rugby competitions. Broadcasting revenue is one of the major sources that all of the Tier One countries rely on. The Islands need to generate and maximise their own revenue streams, and the concept of fielding a team in the Super 14 would give them a real answer: the opportunity to generate or share in broadcasting revenue.

This goal has been embraced by all three unions. If they could achieve this objective (and also possibly inclusion in the SANZAR Tri-Nations competition) and capitalise on the resultant expanded revenue opportunities, the Islands would be in a position to sign their players on professional rugby contracts. This would give the players a solid reason to stay in the Islands. And this equates to tangible optimism about the future.

As a starting point, the Islands are desperate to have their players back in the region so their availability to play international rugby is improved. Tabua makes a strong point: 'At the moment the Pacific Islands don't have the best players playing in their Test matches. Any Tier One nation wouldn't go into a Test match without having their best players available to them.'

The only potentially viable solution according to Tabua is the expansion of the Super 14 competition to either field a Pacific Island team or create the possibility for Pacific Island players to play in the competition with various franchises – while at the same time not jeopardising their eligibility to play for Fiji, Tonga and Samoa. 'Super 14 would be ideal, as it would give the opportunity to play in a regular competition to develop Pacific Islands rugby,' Tabua said.

'If our players could play in a competition in the southern hemisphere it's similar to our Test window, so it would be ideal for us … this would mean having the best players playing at Test level.

'Allowing the Islanders to play in a competition like Super 14 would make it a level playing field.'

So is this a real possibility? What is the potential for SANZAR to include them? CEO of the Australian Rugby Union John O'Neill says he supports the development of Pacific Island rugby but confirms that no decision has been made by SANZAR regarding the future of the Super 14.

'SANZAR is currently engaged in examining future competition structures and at this stage nothing is in and nothing is out,' O'Neill said. 'It is also too early to speculate

on what sort of transformation of Super Rugby might take place.

'As for the Pacific Island nations in isolation, there is no doubt they are an integral part of the international rugby landscape.

'We want the Pacific Islands to be strong and we are keen to investigate ways of assisting their ongoing development in our region.'

But what enticement is there for South African, New Zealand and Australian rugby to put time and energy into changing a successful tournament to develop their poor rugby cousins? The only real upside for SANZAR would be if inclusion of Pacific Islands equals profit. It seems the jury is still out on this. Another hurdle for the Islands is the rule around eligibility, as this has also robbed the Pacific Island nations of some of their best players. Fielea explains: 'Eligibility of players to play for other countries is a problem and the system doesn't really help. For example we have Tongan players who are maybe in Australia or New Zealand and they earn just one cap and then they are not available for the Islands.'

If a player represents another nation at open level in fifteen- or seven-man rugby, even once, this prohibits him from returning to play for his home nation. Currently if an Island player sees hope for a future with a Tier One country, he is willing to jeopardise his eligibility as the potential to earn a sizeable income is too good to ignore. Tabua says that the kids in Fiji look up to those of Fijian origin who play for other nations, such as Wallaby wing Lote Tuqiri and former All Black Joe Rokocoko.

'You see the likes of these players when you are involved in a professional environment and you see what is required ... it will only help the Island nations if they are in that atmosphere and they will pass that on and develop the kids.'

If SANZAR does happen to give them a boost and attempt to genuinely level the playing field and the Islands are to hold their own in this professional era, what is their potential? Tuckey sees continuous top-ten billing in the IRB world rankings as a real possibility.

'Fiji is number nine at present with Tonga and Samoa at twelve and thirteen respectively and they are there despite their lack of resources and the somewhat unique difficulties they each face compared to Tier One unions,' he said.

'Frankly I reckon if each of these unions had the relative resources and advantages of say New Zealand or Australian rugby, they could make top six on the IRB rankings on a regular basis and the combined Pacific Islanders team would beat the Lions if given the opportunity.'

Sons of the Sun
Georgian Rugby on the Rise

by CHRIS THAU

'The "Lelos" … have taken the next step on the ladder after their performance in RWC 2007 and won the European Nations Cup, the so-called "Six Nations B"'

Does anyone remember the closing stages of the RWC 2007 match between Ireland and Georgia, as the 'upstarts' from the Caucasus kept pounding the Irish line, with blood and the scent of an incredible victory in their nostrils? Well, it was not a fluke! Georgia lost, not necessarily because they were the lesser opponent, but because both the odds and history were heavily stacked against them. Ireland, playing Test rugby for more than a century, were expected to shine in the tournament, while the Georgians, who started their international career in earnest in the 1990s, were supposedly there to make up the numbers. In fact, their audacious challenge – combined with the remarkable displays of Tonga, Fiji, and to an extent Romania; not to mention the USA and, yes indeed, the darlings of the public, Portugal – convinced the IRB to retain the 20-nation format for the next RWC, rather than cut down the numbers to 16 as planned. But the day when Georgia will turn the tables on one of the 'grand nations' of the game is not far off.

The 'Lelos', or the 'Sons of the Sun', as they are called (*lelo* is also the name of Georgia's traditional ball game) have taken the next step on the ladder after their performance in RWC 2007 and won the European Nations Cup, the so-called 'Six Nations B', leaving in their trail Russia, Romania and previous holders Portugal. That is no mean achievement with so many of their top players unable to join the national team, due to the restrictive, often illegal, attitude of the French clubs, where the Georgians practise their trade.

The Georgians have been building up gradually since the 1990s, even before the dissolution of the Soviet Union, when they recaptured their much-prized independence. The then secretary of the Georgian union, David Kilassonia, approached the IRB, seeking membership for his yet-to-become-independent union. In 1989 he managed, through an international network of like-minded friends, the seemingly impossible task of bringing Zimbabwe to Georgia for what was the first ever Test match for the newly born rugby nation. In 1992, two years after the Zimbabwe tour, Georgia's yearly fixture list was still limited to a couple of encounters against Ukraine, another by-product of the break-up of the Soviet Union; yet a year later Georgia was able to join the IRB, having meanwhile become an independent republic.

The 1993 qualifying tournament for RWC 1995, held in the northern Polish city of Sopot, when Georgia lost to both Russia and Poland, is regarded as a watershed in the recent history of Georgian rugby. Nearly three years of isolation and civil war had led to a temporary decline in playing standards,

LEFT Goderdzi Shvelidze and Irakli Machkhaneli (from left, facing camera) celebrate Georgia's first try, scored by hooker Akvsenti Giorgadze, in the 30-0 defeat of Namibia at RWC 2007. All three play their club rugby in France.

reflected in the performance in Sopot. The Georgians though disappointed were not disheartened, and having understood the meritocratic nature of the RWC competition went back to the drawing board. They changed the coaching set-up and decided to target the next RWC cycle to make an impact. One of the earliest decisions of the new administration was to employ former Béziers flank forward Claude Saurel to prepare the national team, while at the same time sending the most promising Georgian players to France to fast-track them in a demanding rugby environment.

In addition Zaza Kasashvili, the French-based senior GRU official in charge of player development, strongly supported Saurel's argument – against some powerful opposition from within the traditional Georgian establishment – that the formation of a Sevens squad to play in the newly formed IRB Sevens Series would significantly contribute to the development of Georgian rugby. The players, either at their new French clubs or on the intensely competitive IRB Sevens circuit, absorbed the rugby culture like sponges, making vast progress in a very short time.

RWC 2003 was another step in Georgia's patient but determined effort to reach the top. While they lost all their four matches, they never disgraced themselves in the 'pool of death', which included the future world champions England, South Africa and Samoa. The defeat at the hands of Uruguay was perhaps the most difficult to digest, and ended in acrimony, with the disgruntled public unfairly criticising the players and Saurel for what they perceived as a below-par performance. Saurel left, and for the next RWC cycle Georgian rugby looked inwards and found in three local coaches – former scrum half Malkhaz Tcheishvili, David Chavleishvili and Paata Narimanashvili – the men who took them quite close to the next level, as their near miss against Ireland would testify.

After RWC 2007, which they finished with a flourish against Namibia, probably the most significant step in the recent history of Georgian rugby was the appointment of former Wallaby centre Tim Lane, who boasts an impressive playing and coaching pedigree, as national coach. He became an instant celebrity in Tbilisi. Lane's record speaks for itself: assistant coach of the RWC 1999-winning Wallabies, two stints as Springboks assistant coach under Harry Viljoen and Rudolf Straeuli, head coach of the Cats Super 12 franchise, as well as coach to a number of elite clubs in the French Premiership. His spell in France with Clermont-Ferrand, Toulon and Brive must have come in handy, as most of Georgia's high-profile players play in the French league.

Lane's first match was a hard-fought win over former Continental champions Portugal, followed by success in encounters with Romania and Russia, results that have sent the country's increasingly

RIGHT National coach Tim Lane (in red) watches Georgia against the Emerging Springboks with his assistants Levan Maisashvili and Nikoloz Chavchavadze.

FACING PAGE The Georgian team ahead of the Emerging Springboks game.

large band of supporters wild with anticipation. Lane, aware of the desperate desire for success in his constituency, has asked for patience. 'Teaching a new style, new moves and new calls is a time-consuming business. Of course, the Lelos should stick to their traditional strength, that is vigorous forward play, but at the same time the new, 15-man game will be introduced step by step,' he said.

Georgia arrived at the IRB Nations Cup tournament without most of their high-octane warriors, who were retained by their French clubs, still involved in the final stages of various leagues and championships. Coach Lane was unable to bring to Bucharest about 15 of Georgia's RWC 2007 stars, including Irakli Machkhaneli of Mont de Marsan, Malkhaz Urjukashvili of Aurillac, Akvsenti Giorgadze of Castres, David Zirakashvili and Goderdzi Shvelidze of Clermont-Ferrand. However, their absence was hardly noticed as their replacements did Georgia proud, not only up front but also out wide, the side having adopted a more expansive style since Lane's arrival.

In their first match against the Emerging Springboks, the trophy holders, Georgia put on an impressive performance. Although they lost by a try and two penalties to one penalty (11-3), having held the South Africans to 3-3 at the break, the Georgian players left the field with their heads held high. Add to that the two penalties that hit the South African upright and one has a clearer image of the gallant Georgian challenge in a match of ferocious physical intensity carried on in a remarkable spirit and an atmosphere of total fair play. The Georgians challenged their rivals up front and in the loose, at the rucks and in the mauls. It was relentless and it was brutal, the kind of game the South Africans cherish, and they must be given credit for resisting the onslaught, keeping their cool and emerging winners in the end. Georgia assistant coach Nikoloz Chavchavadze had this to say: 'The match against the Emerging Springboks has tested our young side to the full and we wish to thank our South African friends for the way they played the game, hard but fair. We could have won, but I think that the result is fair; South Africa are the better side and we will learn a lot from the encounter. We will play to win the next match, though in this tournament all teams are of similar standard and anybody can win.'

In the second match the Georgians prevailed 20-18 over a Uruguayan side battling to find both rhythm and match fitness, and in the final game, they simply demolished a very powerful Italy A in a contest more one-sided than the final score of 25-3 dares to suggest. Tim Lane, who departed Bucharest after the first match, leaving in charge his two Georgian assistants Chavchavadze and Levan Maisashvili (both of whom who also coached Georgia U20 to a creditable bronze-medal position in the IRB Junior World Rugby Trophy in Chile), must be delighted with the performance of his young team.

Kiwis Lead the Field
the 2008 Junior World Championship
by ALAN LORIMER

'Behind the scrum, New Zealand used their pace both in attack and defence to leave what had been a classy England back line looking flat-footed'

It came as no shock when New Zealand swept to victory over England at the Liberty Stadium in Swansea to claim the first ever IRB Junior World Championship title. These young All Blacks had shown us their winning formula a year earlier, when they blew South Africa apart in the final Under 19 World Championship in Belfast. Twelve months on, New Zealand were stronger, fitter and faster. The result, it seemed, was inevitable. Indeed, the 2008 Junior World Championship was unique from the perspective of being able to predict (pretty accurately) the likely outcome. From now on, however, there will be no world age-grade tournament at a younger level from which to gauge form, since the Junior World Championship, played at Under 20 level, has replaced both the Under 19 and Under 21 global championships in a welcome rationalisation.

Wales had the privilege of staging this inaugural Under 20 championship and history will surely judge it a success for the Principality. The four venues – Swansea, Cardiff, Newport and Wrexham – all proved popular, the last-mentioned bringing top-class rugby to North Wales as part of the WRU's gospel-spreading work. The hosts, too, could be reasonably satisfied with their own team's performances and their fourth-place finish behind South Africa. But for the Home Unions it was England who carried the flag, the Under 20 Six Nations champions capping a hugely successful season by finishing runners-up to New Zealand and in the process taking the scalps of two southern hemisphere giants, Australia and South Africa.

For England it was the final involvement of their coach, Nigel Redman, who, although disappointed with the final scoreline, praised his players for raising the profile of home rugby. Speaking after the final, Redman said, 'We're very disappointed but this season and this tournament has been awesome for us and we've achieved a lot. We've beaten Australia and South Africa in the last week but New Zealand was a game too far for us.'

England, seeded sixth in the tournament on the basis of their Under 19 placing last year, had little difficulty in swatting aside Canada and Fiji in the first two pool matches, but it was their victory over the highly fancied Australians with a late try from wing Miles Benjamin that rocketed Redman's side into the semi-finals. There, England met South Africa in a contest that was finely balanced until outside half Alex Goode, with a penalty, and prop Alex Corbisiero, with a try, scored the winning points.

The final, however, emphasised the difference between the best of the two hemispheres. New Zealand had the answer to England's heavyweight pack, but in addition to possessing bulk the Under 20 All Black forwards were also much more dynamic, with genuine athletes like skipper Chris Smith at lock leading the way. Behind the scrum, New Zealand used their pace both in attack and defence to leave what had been a classy England back line looking flat-footed, but it was the skill of the Under 20 All Blacks' handling and their willingness to run the ball that gave them their 38-3 win.

As a consequence, expect to see many of the side starring in Super 14 and some progressing to full All Blacks status – players like powerful

FACING PAGE Chris Smith, skipper of the victorious New Zealand side, lifts the IRB Junior World Championship trophy.

BELOW Miles Benjamin of England and Worcester scored two tries against Australia, including a late touchdown to break Wallaby hearts.

prop Ben Afeaki, lock Sam Whitelock, flanker Luke Braid, No. 8 Nasi Manu, who was immense in the final, and just about the whole of the back line, of whom outside half Daniel Kirkpatrick and full back Trent Renata were the pick. It seems New Zealand have a talent production line at which the rest of the world can look with envy.

Yet England, too, can look forward to many of their players bidding for higher honours. As expected, wing Noah Cato was something of a star and Alex Goode looked competent at fly half, as did his number two, Newcastle's Rob Miller, one of several players eligible for next year's contest. Where England might have to change policy is in their pack, which could do with more runners. Bulk will win the majority of matches, but against a side like New Zealand it was ineffective.

South Africa, the other southern hemisphere side to reach the semi-finals, would be disappointed with their final placing, albeit they regrouped to put on a powerful display against Wales in the play-off for third place at the Liberty Stadium. Rediscovering their form after the semi-final defeat to England, they produced a fast, handling game that left Wales trailing 26-6 at half-time. Thereafter the result was inevitable and the 43-18 scoreline a reflection of the gulf between the sides. Earlier, the Junior Boks had looked unbeatable as they scored 108 points against the USA and then put Scotland to the sword with a 72-3 win at Wrexham. But there were signs of cracks when Samoa mounted a physical challenge that all but caused what would have been one of the major upsets of the tournament.

Each team can look back on one great match in the tournament and for Wales it was their win in injury time over an ill-disciplined France side that led 19-9 with only two minutes of proper time remaining. An unsavoury punch-up together with injuries led to extra time being added on, and in the event Wales took full advantage, first with a penalty try and then the winning try and conversion from wing Leigh Halfpenny, to triumph 23-19. Wales will view this tournament as having been an opportunity to expose a number of talented players to a higher level of rugby, and the expectation is that several of their squad will progress, among them centre Jonathan Davies, outside half Daniel Biggar, who will play in next year's tournament, prop Ryan Bevington and No. 8 Sam Warburton.

Positions five to eight in the tournament rankings were sorted out among Australia, France, Argentina and Samoa. The Young Wallabies atoned for their defeat by England to claim fifth place with a 42-21 win over France, while Samoa confirmed their advance up the world rankings at this age level with a 30-10 victory against Argentina.

Less successful were Ireland and Scotland, who met at Newport in the final round to decide ninth place, resulting in a comfortable 39-12 win for Ireland after the Scots had been reduced to 14 men early in the game with the dismissal of wing Tom Bury. Both countries, especially Scotland, lack the numbers to compete seriously in global competitions. Scotland coach Colin Robertson pointed to South Africa's resources, saying, 'Western Province alone have over 100 academy players, we have only 25 in the whole of Scotland and only some of these eligible for Under 20 rugby.'

Ireland fare slightly better than Scotland, but without an increase in playing numbers and a greater intensity in domestic competition for age-level international aspirants, it seems the Scots and the Irish will remain lowly players in global championships.

Italy and Canada fought it out for places eleven and twelve, with the Italians producing their best rugby of the tournament to win 33-10 over a Canadian side that had only narrowly lost 15-10 to Scotland in a fourth-round thriller not decided until late into the second period of extra time.

The last group of four was played out among the countries who finished last in their pools. Tonga triumphed over Fiji 28-20 in the battle of the Pacific Islands to claim thirteenth place, while Japan found their try-scoring rhythm to defeat the USA 44-8 for fifteenth spot. It was a timely win for Japan, who will host the 2009 IRB Junior World Championship. If it is as good as the 2008 tournament in Wales, then stand by for another cracking competition.

BELOW Thiliphaut Marole of South Africa gets a feel for the physical side of Pacific Island rugby against Samoa.

Reach the cultural heart of China with Cathay Pacific.

Fly to over 20 Chinese destinations with Cathay Pacific. Together with our sister airlin
London to China than anyone else. Fly with us and experience award-winning service an
you step on board, to the moment you arrive. To fly Cathay Pacific, call 020 8834 8888, vis

ragonair, we offer more flights from

e warmth of Asian hospitality from the moment

thaypacific.co.uk or contact your travel agent.

CATHAY PACIFIC

Now you're really flying

International Sevens
Hong Kong: Rock 'n' Roll Rugby

by REBECCA BUTLER

'Kenya beat Scotland, which took the Africans to the top of their pool for the first time since 2003, then China produced the shock of the tournament by also beating Scotland'

In 1975 a tobacco company executive and the South African chairman of the Hong Kong RFU were having drinks at the prestigious Hong Kong Club. Whatever was said during their conversation resulted in the birth of the Hong Kong Rugby Sevens. Less than a year later, teams from all over the world took part in the first tournament. In the 1990s demand for tickets was so high that the stadium had to be rebuilt to accommodate a capacity of 40,000. The tournament has continued to

grow and today the Cathay Pacific/Credit Suisse Hong Kong Sevens is widely regarded as the best rugby event, and party, in the world.

This year the tournament celebrated its thirty-second year and I was lucky enough to be there, not only to enjoy the fast, physical Sevens rugby but also to get involved in the rowdy party atmosphere. That's the thing that makes the Hong Kong Sevens different. It is one big multinational celebration of rugby. I made the mistake of sitting in the middle of a row and asked my new friends and fellow spectators to pass me my beer. It was passed through the hands of people from six different nations; some spilt it, some took a sip, but all of them happily helped in getting my drink to me. When it eventually arrived, I contentedly enjoyed my well-travelled – albeit it a bit warm – pint.

The Tens tournament on Wednesday and Thursday before the Sevens has also become very popular and provides good preparation for the main tournament. An event like the Hong Kong Sevens does need a warm-up and you do have to ready yourself for the bright colours, loud music and fierce patriotism. As the pictorial spread on pages 62-63 shows, the costumes are really the main players and this year I was surrounded by Captain Jack Sparrow, gorillas, sumo wrestlers and nurses. I did have to tell the last-mentioned that their costumes would not be very practical in a medical emergency, but looking back I don't think that was the point. The music blasts out between matches and after a team has scored, and the South Stand shakes with raving fans. The lively Cathay Pacific adverts on the big screens also provoke much wild jumping around. It is the spectators themselves, however, who provide most entertainment. A South African man and a Australian woman were having a very heated argument next to me which concluded with her shouting 'Why don't you just go back to your own country?' to which he responded by passionately kissing her, which seemed to go down very well.

The rugby at the Cathay Pacific/Credit Suisse Hong Kong Sevens is so special mainly because there is no elitism – the greats and the not-so-greats all share the same stage for one boisterous weekend. This year there was great excitement and anticipation in the run-up to the tournament as the standing leaders, New Zealand, had not lost a game for almost a year and came to Hong Kong having won the last six IRB Sevens tournaments in a row. South Africa were second in the IRB Series

ABOVE Wales's Gareth Owen grabs Lepani Nabuliwaqa of Fiji during the Pacific Islanders' 15-0 win on day two.

FACING PAGE Rowan Varty of Hong Kong streaks away from the Australian cover on day one. In the end, though, the Wallabies prevailed 24-12.

ABOVE Gabriel Ascarate of the Pumas halts French try scorer Simon Sarthou in the Plate final.

FACING PAGE Alexander Yanyuskin holds aloft the Bowl, successfully defended by Russia.

rankings, and following an aggressive Cup final against New Zealand in San Diego they arrived in Hong Kong prepared to play hard. Samoa also had a point to prove by defending their Hong Kong Sevens title.

The single pool matches on Friday saw wins for the top seeds and the four Six Nations sides present. However, the Asian teams were not to be forgotten and also delivered strong performances, with Hong Kong, Sri Lanka, Japan and Korea being particularly impressive. On day two, Kiwi dominance continued in Pool A with their forward power being the driving force as they stormed into the quarter-finals, scoring an aggregate 85 points against Tunisia and the USA and conceding just one try. The USA finished a respectable second in the pool, although their points difference was not enough to give them a place in the Cup quarter-finals as one of the two best runners-up.

In Pool B England found huge support in the crowd and responded by beating defending champions Samoa. Ben Ryan's young side played well and Ben Gollings' crucial conversion of Simon

Hunt's try gave them the 7-5 win. Meanwhile, Argentine hopes were dashed in Pool C by Renfred Dazel's score for the Boks, despite the Pumas dominating for most of the match. However, the Argentinians did beat Japan 19-5, with the world's leading Sevens scorer, Santiago Gomez Cora, putting his name on the scoresheet. Russia finished third in the group after a win over Japan.

Valiant Welsh defence in Pool D restricted a strong Fijian team to three tries, which was enough to protect Wales's points difference, putting them through to the Cup quarter-finals. Two tries from Lee Williams contributed to their victory over Korea, who were also beaten by Zimbabwe. Pool E brought plenty of shock and surprise. First, Kenya beat Scotland, which took the Africans to the top of their pool for the first time since 2003, then China produced the shock of the tournament by also beating Scotland, 19-12, captain Zhang 'Jonny' Zhiqiang scoring the winning try. China came unstuck against Portugal, however, going down 40-10.

Australia topped Pool F after a close 17-15 victory over Tonga and wins over Hong Kong and France. Tonga avenged themselves after a day one defeat by France with an impressive 56-5 win against Hong Kong. Keith Robertson gave an inspired performance for the host side against France in a 21-21 draw, a result which put Les Bleus out of the Cup competition.

The final day brought yet another exhibition of fantastic rugby, with the crowd still partying hard. It was also yet another day of New Zealand potency that saw them become winners of the Hong Kong Sevens for the first time since 2001. In the final, they got off to the best possible start with an early try for Lote Raikabula, followed by one from Steven Yates. Even though South Africa tried their best to pull the match back, the Kiwis were too good on the day and the final score was 26-12.

The Plate final was a thriller that went into into sudden-death extra time. France dominated the first half against Argentina with tries from Vincent Roux and Simon Sarthou. Argentina responded with a try and then another in the second half, bringing the scores level at 14-14. A drop-kicked penalty goal a minute into extra time saw France clinch the Plate title.

Zimbabwe, back in Hong Kong for the first time in ten years, faced Russia in the Bowl final. The Zimbabweans took the lead in the first half and were ahead 14-7 at half-time. However, the relentless Russians fought back hard in the second half and successfully defended their Hong Kong Sevens Bowl title with a 19-14 win.

What a weekend! The rugby. The city. The people. The party. One not to forget for a lifetime. The Cathay Pacific/Credit Suisse Hong Kong Sevens over for another year and I, for one, cannot wait until next year.

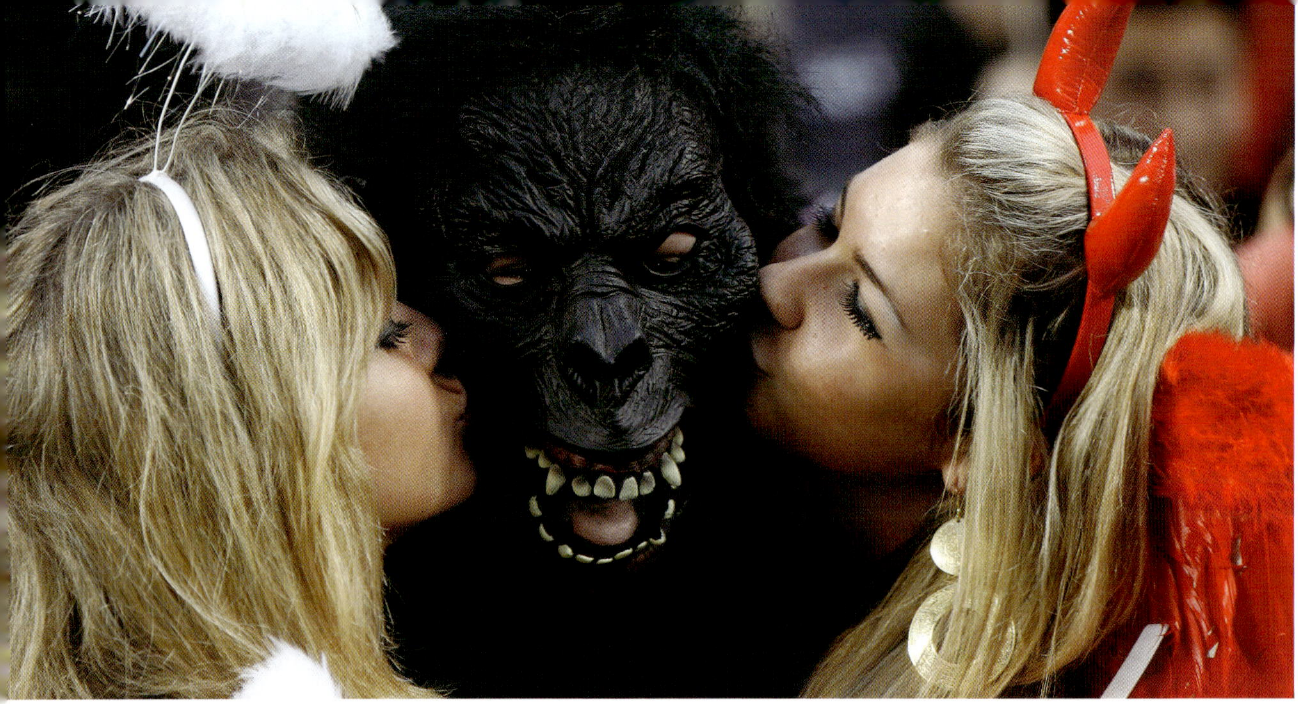

SEVENS
KUKRI
KUKRI

Coke

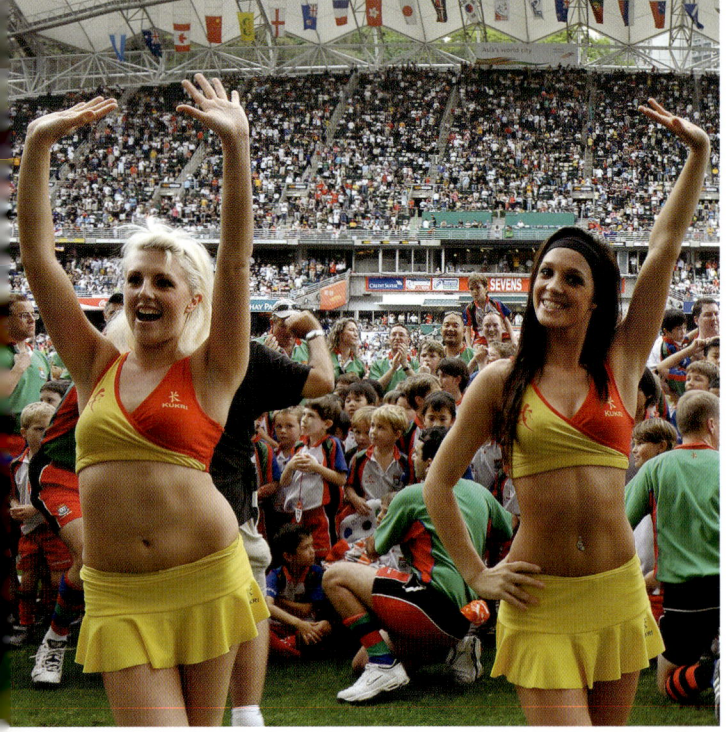

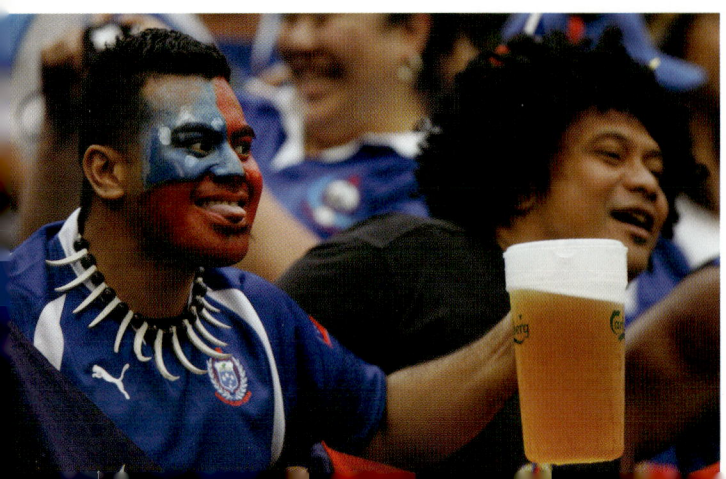

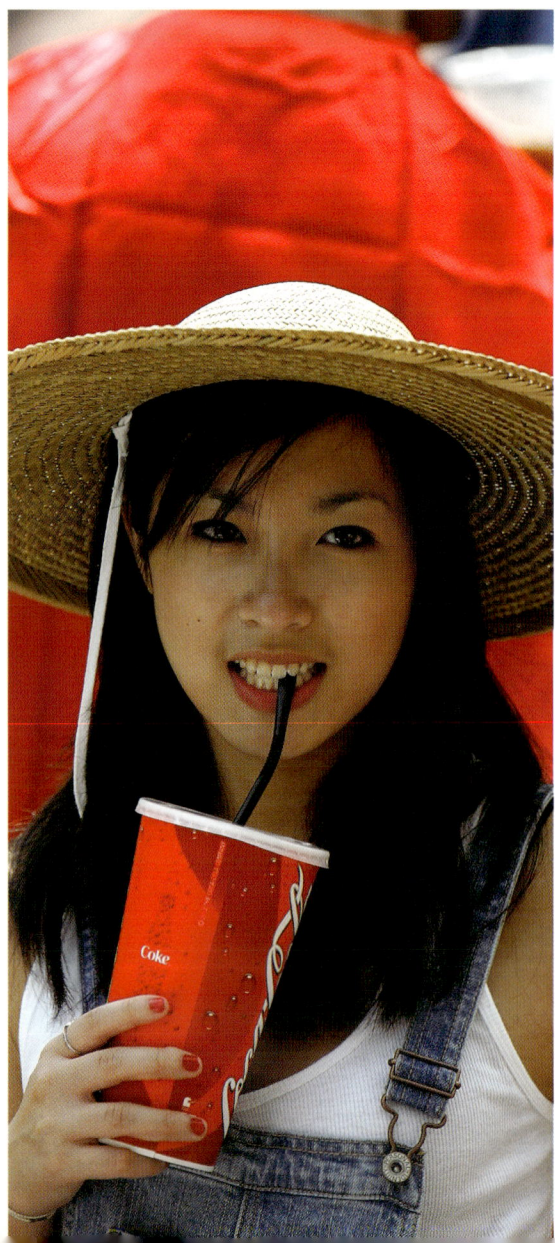

Dubai: Tomorrow the World (Cup) by REBECCA BUTLER

'The first Sevens tournament in the city took place in 1969 at the Dubai Exiles Rugby Football Club and the players were a couple of teams from the local expat community'

Every November, Dubai plays host to the Emirates Airline Dubai Rugby Sevens, arguably the biggest tournament in the IRB Sevens World Series. Players, fans, holidaymakers and locals alike visit the grass pitches and Rugby Village to be part of the internationally renowned rugby carnival. However, 2009 is going to be different. Last year at the Annual Meeting of Council in Dublin, the IRB awarded the fifth Rugby World Cup Sevens to the Arabian Gulf Rugby Football Union, who got the nod ahead of other contenders Australia, Russia, the Netherlands and USA. The tournament will take place from 5 to 7 March and be the first to incorporate a women's competition.

The news was cause for celebration in Dubai, a city with a strong rugby community and a good track record of staging successful Sevens tournaments. That said, hosting a World Cup is playing a very different game and the question had to be asked: would Dubai step up to the challenge? I went to Dubai to meet Gary Chapman, President of Support Services of the Emirates Group, to find out.

Gary told me about the story of the Dubai Sevens. There is so much history attached to the tournament, and its legacy played a big part in the Rugby World Cup 2009 bid. The tournament first started because rugby lovers in Dubai wanted a competition that involved both the game and the traditional social events that go with it. The first Sevens tournament in the city took place in 1969 at the Dubai Exiles Rugby Football Club and the players were a couple of teams from the local expat community. The clubhouse was a Portakabin and the pitches were sand – there was many a grazed knee or skinned elbow! Indeed it was not until the early 1990s that the tournament was played on grass.

The Dubai Sevens gradually evolved and grew to become the tournament it is today. It started to attract good overseas teams – for example, Queensland, Hawke's Bay from New Zealand and charity sides from the UK like The White Hart Marauders. Before the Sevens became an IRB World Series sanctioned tournament, international teams used to participate under different names. Players such as David Campese and Jonah Lomu played in the tournament long before it was an IRB recognised event. In 2007, 160 teams took part, of which only 16 were part of the IRB World Series. The other teams were social teams from around the region – from Dubai, Pakistan, Sri Lanka – as well as invitational teams from all over the globe, including the UK, Continental Europe, Australasia and South Africa. Despite its growth, the Dubai Sevens still holds its customary social functions, such as the Gentleman's Dinner and various other charity events.

LEFT New Zealand are crowned winners of the Emirates Airline Dubai Rugby Sevens 2007, having defeated Fiji 31-21 in the final at the Exiles RFC ground. A spanking new stadium is being built for the 2009 Rugby World Cup Sevens.

When the Emirates Group got involved with the Sevens in 1987, it brought a different perspective to the tournament, which increased the focus on Dubai. The group concentrated on promoting Emirates as an international brand and Dubai as a destination. The company started to invest more in the Sevens and to push international broadcasting and awareness of the tournament (last year, the tournament was broadcast to 120 countries). This promotion accelerated the expansion of the event and encouraged even more people to attend and teams to participate. Emirates wants, in true Dubai fashion, to promote the tournament as a high-quality event; a standard on which the city prides itself. And indeed there are people who visit Dubai for the Sevens alone.

The facilities for the tournament are built from scratch each year, which is no mean feat. Last year, 32,000 people per day attended the Sevens, so stands had to be constructed to accommodate that volume of people, as well as food and beverage outlets and the Rugby Village. It is a major logistical effort; however, one that works. Since the facilities are remade annually, the tournament can grow year on year. The organisers can see what works and what is successful and cater for it the next year. The result of all this is that no two tournaments have been the same.

The Sevens is very important to Dubai. For five years the Dubai Sevens has come top of the poll run in local magazine *What's On* of the area's best sporting events, coming ahead of the Dubai World Cup horse racing, the Dubai Desert Classic golf tournament and the Dubai Tennis Championships. Dubai wants to be a centre of excellence and the sporting capital for the region and rugby is a huge part of that ambition. This is the reason for the World Cup bid and the huge investment in the new facility – to take rugby in Dubai to another level.

RIGHT Danielle Waterman runs away to score against Las Bandidas, as Wooden Spoon defeat the favourites 19-14 in the final to win the 2007 Dubai International Ladies' Sevens Trophy.

FACING PAGE The best pub team in the world? The White Hart Marauders celebrate winning the 1993 Dubai Sevens. From left to right: Paul Johnson, Nick Dyte, Jon Sleightholme, Dave Scully, Damian Hopley, Barry Crawley, Martin Gregory, Chris Sheasby and, in front, Lawrence Dallaglio. The club, formed in 1978, still operates out of the eponymous hostelry in the Hampshire village of Eversley and continues to compete at the highest level in around ten tournaments annually at home and overseas.

But will Dubai be able to cope with stepping up to that level; with the difference between hosting a tournament and a World Cup? The event will be bigger in terms of teams, with 24 men's sides and 16 women's. The tournament will also be very different with regard to atmosphere, as there will be no social teams or events. The attention will be focused solely on the World Cup.

The new stadium is 15 minutes' drive from the old Exiles ground and is three times the size and area. The main pitch will have one permanent stand, capable of seating 4000. This stand will house all the changing rooms and medical and broadcasting facilities, and will have temporary seating for 6000 on top of it. There will be further temporary seating around the remainder of the main pitch, making the total capacity a minimum of 40,000, in comparison with the 32,000 of the old stadium. The pitch is also bigger and has more dead-ball space. A second pitch (of an overall total of six) will be landscaped to create a bowl effect with a grass embankment that can seat up to 10,000. Having two pitches in operation will mean that men's and women's matches can take place at the same time, although all the quarters, semis and finals will be played on the main pitch.

The intention is to create a rugby tournament that has a traditional, country feel to it. It will be a challenge achieving this, mainly because the facilities are being constructed from scratch in the middle of the desert with obvious water and irrigation issues – the nearest water pipeline to the site is 18km away. At the moment, there are not even any roads. There is a great deal of work to be done.

Dubai definitely wants this World Cup, though. They are honoured and feel privileged to be awarded the event. It will not be taken lightly or for granted, and in true Arab fashion of hospitality they will make it work and, furthermore, make a success of it. Everyone will get behind the tournament and there will be a carnival atmosphere in the city. Indeed, one of the main reasons Dubai's World Cup bid was successful was the total support and the commitment displayed by the various municipalities and ministries to deal with the logistical issues that the event will bring.

Dubai's journey along the road to taking its rugby to another level was well under way when the Arabian Gulf was awarded the IRB Rugby World Cup Sevens. Can it succeed and go the whole way? I think it can. After talking to Gary and feeling the growing rugby spirit out there myself, I think Dubai will deliver. There is clearly work to do, but in a city renowned for its hospitality and an increasing love of the game, the World Cup Sevens 2009 in Dubai will be a huge success.

Summer Tours 2008
England in New Zealand

by STEVE BALE

'Thus if he selected creative players, they tended to be physically inadequate; if ... he selected the requisite physical specimens, they were creatively inadequate'

By the end of England's ill-starred venture in New Zealand, Rob Andrew looked and sounded as if he could not wait for the ordeal to end, and – lucky man – it did almost immediately, when Martin Johnson belatedly became the national team manager. To suggest the Test defeats in Auckland and Christchurch were good ones for Johnson to miss as he delayed formally joining the Rugby Football Union payroll is a statement of the blindingly obvious that his stand-in Andrew doubtless communicated long before he arrived back at Twickenham. So Johnson, untainted by guilt even by association, could sit back in Leicestershire after the birth of his son, see what was happening at Eden Park and Lancaster Park, hear about what was happening in various bars and hotels, and attempt to make a fresh start in strategy and even selection, despite his association with the choice to go to New Zealand.

One thing Johnson may remember from his own youth is that boys will be boys, except that when England players are being investigated for alleged rape or sexual assault their conduct – or rather alleged misconduct – has passed beyond the high jinks too familiar from rugby union's amateur(ish) days. So discipline immediately became an issue as serious for manager Johnson, a man with no

formal managerial, let alone coaching, experience when the RFU decided last April to supplant Brian Ashton with the World Cup-winning captain at the head of the England operation.

A ticklish one this, for which Johnson may have felt less prepared than, say, for a Test match in New Zealand (he won in Wellington in 2003, lest we forget). How much latitude should young players, who may act like juveniles but are ostensibly adults, be given to let off steam after Test matches? Andrew said they had to take responsibility for their own actions, which is a truism. Given that when they hit the nightspots of Auckland, they had another Test a week later, not much latitude, you may think, and most of them were on the town again in Christchurch a week later, albeit accompanied by security goons. Yes, it was the end of what had seemed an interminable season, but they had just suffered the second-heaviest England defeat by New Zealand in 103 years.

We can imagine what the All Blacks would have done in such circumstances – stew in their own misery and provoke a national inquest. The Welsh, having lost badly to South Africa in Bloemfontein,

imposed a self-denying ordinance on alcohol and produced a vastly improved performance in their second Test in Pretoria. Spot the difference, then. Johnson undoubtedly did, and if there was one certain consequence of English players' shenanigans in New Zealand it was that Johnson would never again allow them the opportunity so enthusiastically grasped by a relative handful to demonstrate their immaturity and poor professionalism.

So this is one solidly beneficial outcome of three weeks in the Shaky Isles without even beginning to consider what the two matches revealed about those who played or, by omission, those left behind for either rest or recuperation. Naturally England were not helped by the absence of a backs, or attack, coach. But this was a sin of commission and omission

ABOVE Topsy Ojo runs in from 80 metres to score an interception try in the first Test. He later made it a brace on his Test debut.

LEFT Powerhouse All Black centre Ma'a Nonu shreds England's midfield in Auckland.

LEFT The back-row trio of Luke Narraway, here on the charge in Auckland, Tom Rees and James Haskell displayed welcome potential as a unit on the trip Down Under.

FACING PAGE Danny Care delivers the ball during the second Test. The Quins scrum half was another England player to show promise in New Zealand.

by the RFU themselves, because it was they who decided to dispense with Ashton when Johnson became available and were then unable quickly to fill the attack-coach hole they themselves had dug.

Andrew, in one of his last remarks as acting team manager, pointed to the disparity between New Zealand back play and its English counterpart. Thus if he selected creative players, they tended to be physically inadequate; if, on the other hand, he selected the requisite physical specimens, they were creatively inadequate. The latter has normally been the English template. Who cared if they created next to nothing as long as the English pack were shoving it up the opposition – including All Blacks, Springboks and Wallabies – and the ball up their jumpers? Johnson himself was often a devotee of this non-style style, because it was successful.

But what happens when those same opponents combine the two, rather than do an England by having one or the other? We saw the contrasting results of the English either/or, first in Auckland when the midfield channel simply opened up to Ma'a Nonu between Charlie Hodgson and Olly Barkley. Both took the rap by being dropped in Christchurch, but Jamie Noon's inclusion at inside centre with Mike Tindall outside him left England with nothing in midfield with which to threaten New Zealand beyond heavy tackling. As an entirely defensive measure, that could never have won the match. Anyway, England's defence parted even more readily than it had the week before. And think on this – the Blacks have the dazzling Daniel Carter at fly half, but Nonu was well down the list of alternatives before Luke McAlister and Aaron Mauger took themselves to our Premiership.

'From an attacking point of view, clearly there is a physicality around some of the back play that we need to address in our game generally, and some skill elements we need to address too,' Andrew admitted. 'Then there has to be some level of continuity in selection.

'There's no question that we would all be the first to admit we need to get a back line together who stay together for a time and someone working with them regularly. It will come but it takes time.'

Well, quite. Andrew changed virtually his entire back division from Eden Park to Lancaster Park, so he made his own point for himself, and Johnson hardly needed to take note, since one reason his England captaincy was blessed with so many late triumphs in 2003 was that Clive Woodward settled on a team and more or less stuck with it.

Johnson may also have taken note of the false premise on which England's visit to New Zealand was founded, which Andrew repeatedly exposed during that unhappy fortnight. Facing the All

Blacks with 'development' or the next squad selection in mind was a recipe for conclusive defeat. Andrew stated that he, the RFU's elite rugby director, and from afar Johnson needed to look at players in this the ultimate of hostile environments before coming up with the first elite-player squad under the new agreement between the union and Premiership clubs, which started, as did Johnson, on 1 July. By putting it in those terms, it was implicit that what should have been the real objective – the historic glory of beating New Zealand in New Zealand – was unrealisable, even though the haemorrhage of leading All Blacks such as McAlister and Mauger left them unusually vulnerable to an England side supposedly not that far off full strength.

All of this Johnson will by now have marked, learned and inwardly digested, as well as the welcome fact that certain individuals and at least one vitally important unit enhanced reputations which were either ambiguous or non-existent on arrival in New Zealand. The pack matched New Zealand in every area but did not dominate as Johnson's used to, so were not collectively a match-winning force. On the other hand, the English back row of James Haskell, Tom Rees and Luke Narraway handsomely revealed potential – no more, but certainly no less – to become the new Hill, Back and Dallaglio. Narraway's inclusion at No. 8 occurred through the accident of Nick Easter's hand injury, and England were the better for it. He was 24, Rees and Haskell 23, so here were three players with the talent to take England to two World Cups and never mind merely the next one back in New Zealand in 2011. One younger still, Danny Care, 21, has the ability and attitude to become a worthy England scrum half, but this would mean nothing without the personal discipline to exploit himself to the fullest. If ever an individual needed a Johnson talking-to, this was it.

Then there was Mathew Tait, a player messed around by Andy Robinson and Ashton when they coached England but with the moral fibre to recover from everything thrown at him. Even here, he was left on the bench in the first Test. In the second he was the persistent threat England otherwise lacked in either game apart from when Topsy Ojo was chasing kicks or being thrown intercept passes. But Tait is perfectly emblematic of England. He does not always cope so well when the physical stuff is flying, as it invariably does against those Springbok and All Black brutes.

Talking of brutes, it is now down to Martin Johnson to sort out Tait and all the rest. Good luck to him in his new venture, but he will need more RFU support than Robinson and especially Ashton ever had, and a whole lot more fortune. Do you feel lucky, Johnno?

Scotland in Argentina

by ALAN LORIMER

'Aided by a stiff wind at their backs, Scotland roared into a 16-0 interval lead with a try from hooker Ross Ford and three penalties and a conversion goal from Paterson'

If as the sporting cliché would have it 'You're only as good as your last game', then Scotland would have gladly accepted the result of the second Test against the Pumas as an end-of-season judgment on their overall well-being. In a two-Test tour of Argentina, Scotland finished in Buenos Aires by squaring the series and in doing so put behind them much of the misery of their 2007-08 campaign.

The series against Argentina in many ways represented unfinished business. There had been a feeling after the World Cup that Scotland had blown their chances against the Pumas in the Paris quarter-final by adopting a safety-first approach that played into the hands of their opponents. That at least was the perception until the final 15 minutes, when Scotland coach Frank Hadden threw in a batch of replacements to liven up his side's performance.

It worked, as Scotland engineered a fine try from dynamic play – but it was all too late. The damage had been done early on in the game, and Scotland had been forced to settle for another World Cup in which reaching the quarter-finals was the limit of their achievement.

So after a dismal Six Nations, Scotland had only their summer tour to change matters. It was the last chance, too, for Hadden, who, seen as the architect of Scotland's dull approach, was under pressure to perform, not least from his boss, Gordon McKie, the SRU chief executive. McKie had given only a partial endorsement of Hadden by putting him on a rolling contract. Time, it seemed, was running out for the beleaguered coach.

Hadden's preparations for the tour were hampered by not knowing exactly which of his France-based players would be available. In the event, Nathan Hines, Chris Cusiter, Scott Murray, Mark Rennie and Simon Taylor were all ruled out because of French club commitments, while injury robbed the tour party of the Lamont brothers, Scott Lawson, Jim Hamilton and Scotland's erstwhile skipper, back-rower Jason White.

But if the marathon French season affected Scotland, then to an equal extent it determined the Puma squad, the

RIGHT Skipper Mike Blair and his men are justifiably delighted after pulling off a magnificent 26-14 victory over the Pumas in Buenos Aires to square the two-Test series, courtesy of two tries plus 16 points from Chris Paterson's boot.

notable absentees from the Argentina line-up being outside half Juan Martín Hernández and full back Ignacio Corleto.

Hadden, recognising that new blood might help his side out of decline, made several bold selections, among them the inclusion in the squad of the Glasgow pair Thom and Max Evans and the Edinburgh centre Ben Cairns. Crucially, as it was to prove, the Scotland coach made room for Edinburgh outside half Phil Godman, thus making it clear from the outset that he had no intention of playing Chris Paterson in the No. 10 position.

Amongst the forwards, there was a call-up for New Zealander Matt Mustchin, who qualified under the three-year residency rule. The tough lock had shown himself to be a grafter in his three seasons at Edinburgh and seemed the kind of player to take on the Pumas. Elsewhere the late withdrawal of Craig Smith meant promotion for the former Borders prop Geoff Cross, a qualified doctor with ambitions to create a career in international rugby.

Scotland's previous excursion to Argentina had been in 1994, when what was mainly an A side lost the two-Test series by frustratingly narrow margins. Thereafter the Scots suffered two defeats against the Pumas at Murrayfield, in 2001 and 2005, before coming off second best in that 2007

World Cup quarter-final. Scotland's only victory against Argentina had come at Murrayfield in 1990, when they cantered to a 49-3 win. It was a win that was to be savoured because the next one would not come along for a further 18 years.

So with everything to gain after almost two decades without success against the Pumas and with a miserable domestic season behind them, Scotland went into the first Test at the Estadio Gigante de Arroyito in Rosario determined to achieve a result. Hadden named three new caps – centre Ben Cairns, wing Thom Evans and lock Matt Mustchin – in the starting line-up, but while this represented a radical shift for the ultra-cautious Scotland coach, the decision to play Dan Parks signified business as usual.

In the event the Glasgow stand-off gave a now typical display of efficient kicking but offered little to inspire any attacking rugby from the outside backs, in part due to the poor quality of possession provided by the Scottish forwards. As a result, little was seen of Cairns and Evans and overall Scotland rarely threatened their opponents' line.

Yet, despite their pack struggling against the bigger Puma forwards, Scotland put themselves in a winning position when they led 15-10 with some five minutes of playing time remaining. But in a frantic finish, Federico Todeschini kicked two penalty goals for a one-point lead before centre Gonzalo Tiesi exploited a turnover to score in injury time, giving Argentina a 21-15 victory.

Not for the first time all the Scotland points came from the boot of Chris Paterson, who in kicking five goals surpassed the 667 Scottish points record set by Gavin Hastings. Afterwards Paterson famously said, 'I'm proud to achieve the record today, but it's almost embarrassing in the circumstances. I'm massively disappointed that we did not score a try. I've said it time and time again that we need to score tries. We haven't found that formula yet.'

Perhaps Hadden heeded Paterson's remarks as he mulled over selection for the second Test along with his assistants, Andy Robinson, the former England coach now heading up Edinburgh, and Sean Lineen, the Glasgow head coach. It was a bolder selection, particularly behind the scrum and crucially at fly half, where Phil Godman returned from the cold to replace the much-criticised Parks. Paterson, used to being shunted from position to position in the Scotland side, was picked at left wing, with Simon Webster on the opposite beat and Hugo Southwell at full back. In the pack there was a strong Andy Robinson influence with the inclusion at open-side flanker of John Barclay to beef up the physical contest at the breakdown.

LEFT Chris Paterson holds up Bernardo Stortoni in the first Test in Rosario, in which the Scotland back passed Gavin Hastings' national points-scoring record.

FACING PAGE Centre Graeme Morrison heads for the posts to score Scotland's second try in their victory in Bueno Aires.

The Scots had prepared much better for the second Test and were confident going into the game at Estadio José Amalfitani in Buenos Aires, despite facing a Puma side strengthened by the return of several France-based players. Significantly, too, Scotland opted for a high-tempo game, thus avoiding strength-sapping confrontations with the muscular Puma pack.

Godman, deservedly back in the side after a good season with Edinburgh, is not the complete playmaker, but with him in charge at stand-off, the Scotland outside backs were able to play at pace. Aided by a stiff wind at their backs, Scotland roared into a 16-0 interval lead with a try from hooker Ross Ford and three penalties and a conversion goal from Paterson.

Even playing into the breeze, Scotland were able to extend their lead with a further Paterson penalty, but then came the inevitable Puma backlash with a converted try from Ignacio Fernandez Lobbe. With Argentina stepping up the pressure, Scotland then struck lucky as Parks, after coming off the bench, intercepted before sending Graeme Morrison in for a try under the posts, converted by Paterson. But in injury time Argentina clawed back seven points with a try by Horacio Agulla, converted by Todeschini. This late score brought the final reckoning to 26-14, shortening the winning margin to below the 16 points Scotland needed to overtake Ireland and reclaim eighth spot in the IRB world rankings, crucial to the 2011 World Cup draw.

Still, this was the result that Scotland and Hadden had sought. The coach had regained some lost ground, and his players had proved to themselves that they could replace the stultifying style they showed in the Six Nations with an exciting brand of rugby. Moreover, where Wales and Ireland had failed in recent years, Scotland had managed to tame the Pumas in their own backyard.

In terms of personnel, Evans, Cairns and Mustchin all came through their international baptisms, Morrison looks to have re-established himself at inside centre, while Godman showed that his game can raise the tempo of Scotland's attack. At open-side, Barclay impressed when given his chance in the second Test, while Scott MacLeod's consistently high standards suggest that the Scarlets lock might be moving into contention for Lions selection.

Wales in South Africa

by GRAHAM CLUTTON

'Wales had shown glimpses of their rejuvenation, courtesy in particular of one or two moments of genius from ... Shane Williams ... Gareth Cooper and ... Jamie Roberts'

It was supposed to be the definitive showdown between the best in Europe and the world champions – Wales, the deserved Grand Slam winners and a side who had developed out of all recognition since the arrival of Warren Gatland and Shaun Edwards, against a Springboks side who under new coach Peter de Villiers had chosen a new pathway in the wake of their World Cup victory under the guidance of Jake White.

In the end, Wales's two-match summer tour to South Africa was not what it might have been. Admittedly the Springboks can claim to have once again put one over on the frontrunners of European rugby. However, with injury problems suffered prior to the June excursion having significantly diluted the strength of Gatland's tour party, any hopes Wales might have had of beating the Springboks on South African soil for the first time had all but disappeared by the time the squad touched down in time for the first Test in Bloemfontein. Even so, by the time the final whistle was blown in Pretoria a week later, Wales had shown glimpses of their rejuvenation, courtesy in particular of one or two moments of genius from wing Shane Williams, scrum half Gareth Cooper and Cardiff Blues utility back Jamie Roberts. More importantly, though, while their immediate hopes and expectations had been dashed through no fault of their own, the overall experience made clear down exactly which road this particular Wales side needs to travel in the coming months.

To their credit, the Six Nations champions overcame the disappointment of their 43-17 first Test defeat to push the Springboks significantly closer in the second Test in Pretoria. Gatland's men led going into the final quarter, but in the end the Springboks pulled away to record a 37-21 victory – a final scoreline that was harsh on their opponents. Coach Gatland said, 'If we are going to close the gap, then the key for us is to win against the southern hemisphere sides. First, we have to achieve that in a home game and after that, we must raise the bar and do it away.

'I am mindful of my experiences when I was at Wasps that that's what England did. When they won the World Cup in 2003, they tried to play the southern hemisphere teams as often as they could.

'Winning at home at Twickenham gave them the initial confidence and then they went on to win away from home. They got into that winning habit and when they went to Australia for the World Cup, they had enough confidence and know-how to win it.

'If we've got an ambition to do that and get better as a team, then that's the progression we've got to take as a side.

RIGHT Wales scrum half Gareth Cooper puts boot to ball during the first Test in Bloemfontein as Springbok forwards Juan Smith and Bakkies Botha look on.

FACING PAGE South Africa's Jean de Villiers claims his second, and his team's third, try of the second Test against Wales in Pretoria. The centre also made the scoresheet in Bloemfontein.

'As far as this tour was concerned, we know we had some key players that weren't available and that obviously affected us.

'I think the players who came out on tour will have learned a massive amount over the last two weeks and as coaches we've learned a lot too.

'We say we want to keep improving as a side and all along our goal has been to be a good side in a couple of years' time and I think we are on the right track in terms of our progress.'

Gatland was delighted with the character shown by his players in the second Test as they bounced back from a mauling in Bloemfontein. Tries from Roberts and Shane Williams had kept Wales in touch for a time in that opening game, but the Springboks were far too strong at forward, and any hopes of success in the match were soon dashed as the South Africans scored four tries through full back Conrad Jantjes, centre Jean de Villiers, No. 8 Pierre Spies and replacement centre Percy Montgomery. In the second Test, though, it was a different story altogether, with first-half tries from Gareth Cooper and Shane Williams plus 11 points from the boot of outside half Stephen Jones giving Wales a 21-20 lead with a quarter of the match remaining. Sadly, it was an all too familiar story in the last 20, with de Villiers and Bismarck du Plessis crossing for late tries to make sure that there was to be no first win for Wales on Springbok soil.

FACING PAGE Shane Williams' purple patch continued, the Wales wizard scoring two brilliant tries, one in each Test.

BELOW Springbok full back Conrad Jantjes flies in to open South Africa's try account in Bloemfontein, where the world champions defeated the Grand Slam winners 43-17.

'I was proud of their efforts,' said Wales assistant coach Edwards. 'The players showed a massive amount of maturity after the first Test and were truly very disappointed with the result.

'They went out for something to eat on the Saturday night in Bloemfontein and made a call themselves that they wouldn't have a beer because they wanted to lift this performance.

'I was really proud of the way they lifted themselves from the disappointment of the previous week and the manner in which they came out and performed with some credit.

'I still think on the day the better team won. But there were a couple of shots at goal we missed, which at this level you've got to take, and I was pretty aggrieved with some of the decisions.'

In particular, he was unhappy with a critical call that didn't go Wales's way under the Springboks' posts after Alun-Wyn Jones burst through ten minutes into the second half. 'When the ref says there's a knock-on when you can clearly see there's a hand in there, it's pretty frustrating,' he said. 'You feel like if that had been at the other end, it would have been a penalty the other way and a yellow card.

'I know Stephen Jones was also frustrated with the first try Jean de Villiers scored, as he felt the referee got in the way and he wasn't able to make a tackle. I said the next time it happens, make sure you smash the referee out of the way!'

However, all round, it was a performance that provided Gatland and co. with justified reason to look ahead with hope and expectation. Gatland added, 'No disrespect to some of the other teams in the Six Nations, but I think if we had've been playing another Six Nations team we would have won the second Test quite comfortably.

'I would have been happy to have stayed out there for another ten weeks playing this team, because that's only going to make us a better side and we desperately want to be a better side.'

Edwards shares Gatland's overall satisfaction and his prediction of a bright future for the squad and the national game in Wales. 'I think the second Test was more of a true reflection of us as a team and the guys can hold their heads up high,' said Edwards.

'We took them on and it could have gone either way after 60 minutes. I think a nine- or a five-point scoreline to the Boks is probably about where we are at the moment.'

The individual success stories were, without doubt, Shane Williams and Jamie Roberts, the latter further confirming his emergence as one of the game's most exciting young players.

However, as for winning on southern hemisphere soil – well, Wales will have wait for another season at least.

Because every project presents unique demands, we work closely with
clients to understand their objectives. We offer in-depth industry knowledge,
delivering practical solutions and clear strategies aimed at making the deal work.

With commitment and innovation "clients are impressed with the team's level of creativity".†

With an integrated network of leading individuals, Clifford Chance's International
Real Estate Group has the commitment, resources and know-how to get deals done,
whatever and wherever they are.

For more information please visit **www.cliffordchance.com/real estate**

† Chambers & Partners Europe 2007

C L I F F O R D
C H A N C E

www.cliffordchance.com

Ireland Down Under

by SEAN DIFFLEY

'It was a horrendous day weatherwise, as the rain pummelled down in biblical quantities accompanied by a predominantly southerly wind that never quite made up its mind'

Down Under is not the happiest backpacking venue for the Irish rugby team. Not since Ollie Campbell produced a magical kicking demonstration in 1979 have Ireland beaten Australia; and in the 103 years since the Donegal-born Dave Gallaher led the first All Black tour north, the Irish have never beaten New Zealand – the 21-11 defeat in Wellington in 2008 was the twentieth, with a 10-10 draw at Lansdowne Road in 1973 the closest call so far.

It was a horrendous day weatherwise, as the rain pummelled down in biblical quantities accompanied by a predominantly southerly wind that never quite made up its mind as to its exact course. However, its origin was the Antarctic, as the many suffering from hypothermia readily attested. Despite these conditions and the fact that the Irish were playing in their fifty-third week, they could, with a bit more luck and a few less errors, have managed a win.

ABOVE Daniel Carter is brought up short by Jamie Heaslip and Tommy Bowe in Wellington, but Ireland were unable to record a first win against the All Blacks.

ABOVE Centre Paddy Wallace slides in for a try to put Ireland 8-5 up with 22 minutes played.

FACING PAGE Wallaby James Horwill makes a spectacular take against Ireland at Melbourne. The lock, making only his second appearance for Australia, also scored one of his side's two tries in the game.

It was 8-8 at half-time with Ireland's points coming from a Ronan O'Gara penalty goal and a splendid midfield break by centre Paddy Wallace for a try. New Zealand had a try from flying wing Sitiveni Sivivatu and a penalty from the inevitable Dan Carter. Brian O'Driscoll drifted out to allow Conrad Smith beat him on the inside to pave the way for his winger's try. O'Driscoll played manfully, particularly in defence, but he is a shade less in quality than he was a couple of seasons ago. As television pundit Scott Quinnell wisely remarked, 'Brian has had too much rugby, too many hamstring problems. He should really go away for a few weeks and just fish or something.'

The seven Munstermen in the pack, aided and abetted by the Leinster back-row Jamie Heaslip, performed well in all the circumstances, with Paul O'Connell at his outstanding best. But there were some mistakes at the line outs, and in the last few moments crucial errors entered Irish procedures when there was a definite chance of winning. Marcus Horan, the loose-head prop, had a bang at an All Black, and instead of an Irish scrum which referee Chris White had awarded, it became a successful Dan Carter penalty goal. O'Connell's glare at Horan was worth a thousand words.

Midway through the rain-and-wind-lashed second half, O'Gara gave Ireland an 11-8 lead with a penalty, but Carter equalised. Yet it was still all to play for until Horan's silly error, which put the All Blacks 14-11 ahead. Until then, New Zealand were certainly vulnerable despite their power up front and the inspirational play of Richie McCaw. Just into the final quarter, Wellington centre Ma'a Nonu went over for a converted try, taking the score to 21-11 to the All Blacks, where it stayed. It could be argued that this scoreline flattered New Zealand's overall display a bit. Although their forwards were more powerful than their Irish counterparts, they were not able to dominate as in games of yore, and individual flashes of brilliance from Carter and McCaw were really the deciding factors.

A week later, Melbourne's Telstra Dome was closed, so conditions were so different from Wellington in this Test, won by Australia 18-12. Once again, the Irish could have won and in the final moments mounted a thrilling attack of 18 phases as they drove at the Aussie line. It ended with a spilled ball, and the exhausted players of both sides collapsed on the ground as the final whistle blew – the Wallabies, because they had tackled themselves to a virtual standstill; the Irish, because their season had started 12 months before and they were, as described earlier, knackered.

Robbie Deans, the new Wallabies coach, was no doubt very pleased at the quality of his side's defence. Ireland had the majority of possession but in a fast and entertaining game failed to register enough on the scoreboard. Australia led 15-7 at half-time, with the new half-back combination of scrum half Luke Burgess and out-half Matt Giteau combining effectively. The star of the Irish side was young full back Robert Kearney, whose forays in midfield and ability to sidestep and progress so entertainingly augurs well for the future. Luke Fitzgerald, another promising young prospect, was injured in early training and took no part in the tour. The Irish points came from tries by Denis Leamy and Brian O'Driscoll and a conversion from Ronan O'Gara. Australia in reply scored tries through centre Berrick Barnes and lock forward James Horwill, Giteau converting one and also kicking two penalty goals.

Although next season Ireland will have a new coach in Declan Kidney, Michael Bradley of Connacht took charge for this tour Down Under and by all accounts acquitted himself very well. Kidney's arrival in post was postponed until after the tour so that he could see Munster through the Heineken Cup final, which they won. He still travelled south, though, with new Irish manager Paul McNaughton, the pair confining their visit to viewing the matches and consulting with New Zealand and Australian coaches about the new laws that will be in force next season.

Churchill Cup

by HUGH GODWIN

'[The Saxons'] style of play was high-tempo with rapid offloads, and if it did not always work, it was a departure from that seen in senior England sides of late'

The Barclays Churchill Cup has become a summer staple in the increasingly eclectic genre of cross-border tournaments supported by the International Rugby Board and, unsurprisingly, the winners wore the white jerseys of the England Saxons. The second-string representatives of the Rugby Football Union – co-organisers of the tournament with Rugby Canada and USA Rugby – took the title for the fourth time in six years.

The Saxons defeated Scotland A in the Cup final at Chicago's Toyota Park, the handsome 20,000-seater home to the Chicago Fire soccer team, where David Beckham had strutted his stuff for the LA Galaxy a few months previously. The rugby men drew a crowd of 9434 spectators, who enjoyed a triple-header that also comprised the Plate final, between Ireland A and Argentina A, and the Bowl final – a full Test which carried IRB ranking points – between the USA and Canada.

Choosing the Windy City as the thirteenth different venue for Churchill Cup matches since 2003 conjured exciting thoughts of skyscrapers and Al Capone mingled with a little Roxie Hart. The reality, though, was more prosaic: only a single time zone separated Chicago from the small wedge of Canada – Ottawa, Kingston and Toronto – where the six pool matches were held, so the logistics were much more sensible than for the 2006 event, which all but spanned North America.

Argentina A returned to the Churchillian mix in place of 2007 runners-up New Zealand Maori, who were otherwise engaged in the Pacific Nations Cup. The shadow Pumas went into Pool A with Scotland A and Canada; England Saxons and Ireland A made up Pool B together with the USA, who were in the charge of Scott Johnson, former backs coach to Wales and Australia.

Saxons head coach Steve Bates was assisted by the rising star of London Irish forwards coaching, Toby Booth, and line-out specialist Simon Hardy. This trio and their tour captain, Harlequins flanker Will Skinner, presided over a fairly straightforward 64-10 thumping of the USA in the tournament

opener at Twin Elm Rugby Park in outer Ottawa. England scored nine tries, three of which went to Matt Banahan, the gigantic Jersey-born lock-turned-wing, who was quickly into his enormous stride. An eagerness to get the ball to Banahan cost the Saxons an interception try by Gavin DeBartolo, and the USA were 24-7 down at half-time. Six further tries after the break – including Banahan's third, plus a penalty try after 69 minutes when the USA scrum imploded, and a 70-metre dash by replacement wing Ugo Monye – helped ram the Saxons' superiority home.

Each of the three rounds of pool matches consisted of a double-header, and the first Pool A game followed the Saxons-USA encounter in Ottawa, the Scots kicking off with a 26-10 win over Canada. This was Steve Jones's match. The 25-year-old Northumberland-born Newcastle full back had played for England Under 19 before switching allegiance to Scotland at Under 21 level; he also dabbled in rugby league with Huddersfield Giants. Here Jones displayed a canny positional sense, and collected three tries. 'I always felt full back is my strongest position even though I have played a bit at 10 and 12,'

he said. Centre Calum MacRae was the Scots' sole survivor from the team coached by none other than Bates that had beaten the Saxons in Toronto in 2006.

The tournament then moved south to the Richardson Stadium in Kingston, Ontario, where Wednesday's pair of matches were chalk and cheese. Scotland A edged out Argentina A 27-24 to win Pool A and secure a place in the Cup final. Fly half Gordon Ross's penalty goal was, in simplistic terms, the difference. Then the USA fell with another heavy bump, defeated 46-9 by Ireland A, who were captained from the second row by Bob Casey of London Irish. They also had substantial back-row resources in Neil Best, Roger Wilson, Johnny O'Connor and David Pollock. To call these four combative would be like describing the CN Tower in Toronto – third stop on the pool itinerary – as a lamp post on the shores of Lake Ontario. But Ireland A would be undone by the tiringly quick turnaround between pool matches from Wednesday to Saturday, when they met England Saxons in warm and humid conditions at Fletcher's Fields in Toronto, and ultimately it hurt.

England were flustered in the 10th minute by a quick line out and a hoisted kick that led, aptly enough, to the Garryowen centre Keith Earls bulleting through for a try. But the Saxons replied with Steffon Armitage of London Irish – starting at open-side instead of Skinner – setting up a ruck from which scrum half Paul Hodgson's box kick was brilliantly claimed by Anthony Allen. The Gloucester centre jinked to the 22, gave a deft pass to the supporting Hodgson, and the scoring pass, almost inevitably, went to Banahan.

ABOVE Bath's giant wing Matt Banahan proved something of a handful, scoring three times against USA, twice against Ireland A and a sixth try in the Cup final against Scotland A.

FACING PAGE Scotland A's Colin Gregor, who also scored in the Cup final, crosses here in the 27-24 victory over Argentina A.

The Saxons pressed on to win 34-12, with the bleached-blond thatch of back-rower Jordan Crane prominent. Their style of play was high-tempo with rapid offloads, and if it did not always work, it was a departure from that seen in senior England sides of late. Crane's charges across the gain line recalled Lawrence Dallaglio in his pomp; if the young Leicester forward can add the wide range of Dallaglio's passing and support play, he could go far. Earls's second try was just a blip as the Saxons crossed five more times through Armitage, Monye, Banahan again, Allen and Nick Abendanon, the Bath full back who had been a whisker away from World Cup selection the previous autumn.

In the second game at Fletcher's Fields, Argentina A went nip and tuck with Canada before prevailing 17-16, so, with a week to recuperate, it was on to Chicago. The England players stayed in Burr Ridge, about 30 minutes' drive from downtown. Some went fishing, others swam from the beach on Lake Michigan. While in Toronto, the squad's American sports enthusiast, George Chuter, had led a visit to the Blue Jays' baseball batting practice, and now a few players went to a White Sox game. Yes, there were elements here of the tours of yore.

But everyone had eyes on the Churchill Cup prize, and with live satellite TV coverage both sides of the Atlantic, the Saxons and Scots played out an entertaining quasi-Calcutta Cup. The 6ft Jones was the shortest of Scotland's five outside backs. England had Chris Robshaw of Harlequins at blind-side alongside Crane and the restored Skinner. The consistent Chris Jones of Sale and Wasps' George Skivington made up the second row. This was not one for the faint-hearted. The Saxons led 16-9 at half-time, Gloucester fly half Ryan Lamb having kicked three penalties and the conversion of Banahan's 25th-minute try, for which Monye made the extra man in midfield behind a scrum and Crane, Ollie Smith and Allen prised open the Scottish defence.

During the interval Booth exhorted England to keep the ball and let the heat do the rest. The Scots initially refused to play ball. Their centre Rob Dewey executed a nice scissors with Ross and shrugged off Crane and Allen to make a try for Glasgow scrum half Colin Gregor, and a penalty apiece by Ross and Lamb made it 19-19. But the Saxons finished strongly. A Scottish overthrow at a line out was punished by Lamb, who spotted a dog-leg in the onrushing defence and passed long to Abendanon, who scored. Crane reprised the triumphant touch-line sprint of his clubmate Tom Croft in the Twickenham final a year before, then came the concluding act in the Saxons' 36-19 victory: a cross-kick from Lamb to Monye, who brushed off Gregor for the fourth English try. Banahan had six overall to finish as the competition's top try scorer.

In the other finals, Ireland A defeated Argentina A 33-8 to take the Plate, and Canada – coached by Kieran Crowley, the former All Black full back – earned North American bragging rights with a 26-10 win over the USA. Overall the 2008 Churchill Cup came out sunny side up, partly due to its place early in the four-year World Cup cycle. Players on all sides knew there were senior places there to shoot for and it made for a positive attitude 'on tour'. Next year's Churchill Cup will be exclusively in the USA as the organisers strive to both consolidate and innovate.

You'll be converted

once you see how we go to the ends of earth and beyond to give you the best property advice in Scotland

Culverwell
PROPERTY CONSULTANTS

HOME FRONT

SCOTLAND'S FINEST FLY HALF.

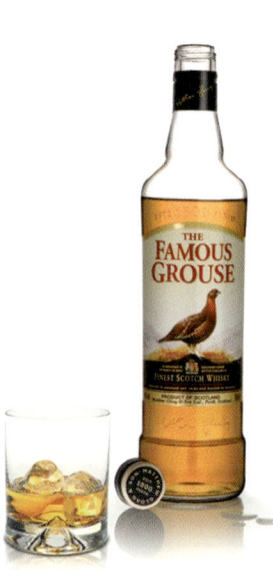

Wasps Dig Deep the 2007-08 Guinness Premiership

by CHRIS HEWETT

'Lest we forget, there was a World Cup taking place in the autumn of 2007, and when World Cups happen these days, they happen to Wasps more than to any other team in England'

It is tempting to believe now that Wasps were always going to recapture the Guinness Premiership title they let slip from their grasp in 2006, when Sale upset the apple cart by winning the title from a position at the top of the regular-season table, rather than down amongst the also-rans. The coaching partnership of Ian McGeechan and Shaun Edwards was reaching full flower; the flankers James Haskell and Tom Rees had another year's hard yakka behind them and were ready to perform like true international forwards; two southern hemisphere types, the high-class centre Riki Flutey and the born-awkward prop Pat Barnard, had joined the club. And then there was that Dallaglio chap, jaw-jutting his way through his sixteenth and final top-flight season. Lawrence was bound to bow out on a winning note, wasn't he? It was written in the stars, the tea leaves, and just about everywhere else.

Of course, it was not like that at all. Lest we forget, there was a World Cup taking place in the autumn of 2007, and when World Cups happen these days, they happen to Wasps more than to any other team in England. Certain rivals were heavily affected by the global gathering – Bath lost most of their top-drawer tight five to England, as well as Olly Barkley, their principal source of points; Leicester, the reigning champions, contributed great swathes of forwards to the tournament, not to mention backs of the calibre of Geordan Murphy, Dan Hipkiss, Seru Rabeni and Alesana Tuilagi; Gloucester suddenly found themselves without such influential figures as Carlos Nieto and Marco Bortolami. But Wasps were stripped bare. Dallaglio began the season in France rather than High Wycombe, and he took Josh Lewsey, Eoin Reddan,

RIGHT Man of the Match Simon Shaw of Wasps nails Leicester skipper and former England team-mate Martin Corry during the 2007-08 Guinness Premiership final at Twickenham.

Raphaël Ibañez, Phil Vickery, Simon Shaw, Joe Worsley, Dan Leo and the open-side specialist Rees with him across the Channel. Wasps did not have the biggest squad to start with. Now, they were left with the smallest one.

Things might easily have been worse. Brian Ashton, the head coach of England, could – indeed should – have taken Haskell as well. The mesmerising Danny Cipriani would also have added value, although that became clearer with hindsight. McGeechan was relieved to hang on to those two, and must have been happier still when the back-row forward John Hart, underrated outside the immediate club environment but never undervalued within it, revealed himself as a natural leader. Even so, Wasps won only two of their first eight Premiership matches. By Christmas, they were still stuck in the foothills and struggling to find a way up.

The likes of Gloucester were much happier. Dean Ryan's team, armed with that golden generation of bright young things in the back division, went at it from the 'b' of the 'bang', scoring so heavily in their early outings that the popular pre-season predictions of Cherry and White domination seemed well rooted in fact, as well as logic. They won their first five games, accumulating at the very handsome rate of 35 points a time. In the opening round of fixtures, an unusually substantial wing called Lesley Vainikolo – a Tongan who had played rugby league for New Zealand and would soon declare himself available to play union for England on residency grounds – put five tries past Leeds. Two things were immediately clear: Vainikolo was not the sort to give a sucker an even break, while Leeds were bottom-of-the-table fodder.

If Vainikolo found life more difficult when he ran out of seven-stone weaklings to thump around – his performances for England marked him down as one of sport's 'flat-track bullies' – Leeds did nothing to alter the early perception that they would quickly be redespatched to National League One. After a rough start, they improved in early October to push Newcastle close at Kingston Park. A week later, they beat Worcester at Headingley. A glimmer of hope? Not really. Despite the best efforts of their admirably loyal wing Tom Biggs and their ultra-reliable captain Stuart Hooper, they would not win again in the Premiership until late March.

Worcester were in a strange place for much of the campaign. After retaining their Premiership status by the last layer of skin on their teeth the previous spring, they had dispensed with the services of John Brain, reputed to be one of the best analysts in the European game, and recruited Mike Ruddock, who had led Wales to a Grand Slam in 2005 before falling victim to dark deeds in the lair of the Red Dragon. Sam Tuitupou, an excellent inside back from New Zealand, had already agreed a move to Sixways, and he was followed by two other recent All Blacks, the lock Greg Rawlinson and the stellar wing Rico Gear. It seemed for all the world as if Cecil Duckworth's generous investment in West Midlands rugby would begin to pay dividends – that Worcester would leave life in the bottom half of the table behind them and push hard for Heineken Cup qualification.

None of this happened. By round 11, Worcester had only a single draw to show for their efforts, and while they beat Bristol at Sixways in late January, they had to wait another month to really spark their season into life with a fine victory at Sale. The saving grace was their collection of losing bonus points. Unlike their relegation rivals from Yorkshire, the Midlanders were competitive against all-comers. They were finishing second, but not by much, and as Tuitupou and Rawlinson started to make their presence felt, their fortunes improved. Meanwhile, Gear, extraordinarily, would struggle for a starting place, thanks to the successful rehabilitation of Marcel Garvey on one wing and the emergence of the brilliant Miles Benjamin on the other. By the time the win at Sale lifted their spirits – they would go on to beat Leicester, Gloucester, Bristol and Newcastle, as well as reach the final of the European Challenge Cup – Worcester's worst fears had eased.

For the first time in several years, then, interest was concentrated at the top end of the table, not the bottom. And it was not a case of the usual suspects, either. Saracens, intelligently coached by the Australian wiseacre Alan Gaffney, won six of their first eight games, drawing on the effective half-back partnership of Neil de Kock and Glen Jackson. Consumed by their unlikely success in the Heineken Cup – their quarter-final victory over the Ospreys at Vicarage Road was one of the highlights of the campaign, not least because it marked the late autumnal blossoming of Richard Hill's wonderful career as a flanker for all the ages – they would fall away in the latter stages, but they did enough to suggest that

BELOW Olly Barkley cannot stop James Simpson-Daniel from crossing for the only try of Gloucester's 8-6 win over Bath at Kingsholm in the final round of the regular season.

Gaffney's replacement, another super-smart Australian by the name of Eddie Jones, has strong foundations on which to build.

Harlequins, equally well prepared by Dean Richards, the Great Shambling Bear of the English game, also made a decent start and lasted rather longer. One of their loose forwards, occasional captain Nick Easter, was a first-pick player for England at the World Cup, yet by the end of the season, he was struggling for a place in the starting line-up at club level as a new Quins back-row unit took shape. Chris Robshaw's work rate in the No. 6 position won him plaudits from all points of the compass; Will Skinner's enthusiastic approach to the rough-and-tumble breakaway duties resulted in man-of-the-match awards by the gross; and Tom Guest, quick and classy at No. 8, set tongues wagging as Quins closed in on the top-four finish of their dreams.

They would have made it, too, but for a compelling last round of regular-season fixtures in early May. Gloucester were already guaranteed a place in the play-offs, despite some scratchy performances away from Kingsholm. (Their victory at Wasps in round 21 came straight out of the wide blue yonder.) Bath, meanwhile, were running hot under Steve Meehan, who had developed a high-octane offloading game that suited the likes of Matt Stevens, Michael Lipman and the two South African half backs, Michael Claassens and Butch James. The two West Country clubs met on Cherry and White land and produced one of the games of the year: a one-try, fourteen-point extravaganza of fast, hard, ferociously committed rugby that proved, as if proof were needed, that the thrust of the International Rugby Board's experimental law variations was wrong-headed and ill-conceived. Gloucester won, just, to finish top.

By winning with a bonus point at Leeds, Wasps found their way into second. They had set themselves up for a high finish some weeks before by beating Bath at the Recreation Ground in another spellbinding contest. McGeechan and Edwards feared defeat that day would scupper their chances of another late charge into play-off contention, and that fear of failure manifested itself in the nature of the Wasps performance. Bath helped them out with some sloppy defence after the interval, but the performances of Cipriani, Haskell and the ever-dependable Hart were wonders to behold. From there on in, the Londoners would win nine matches out of ten.

So, while Gloucester and Bath were going at it hammer and tongs in front of 16,000-plus supporters at Castle Grim, and Wasps were doing a thoroughly professional job on Leeds at Headingley, the real fun and games was taking place in Stockport and Leicester. Sale had only to beat London Irish to secure themselves a semi-final spot, and judging by their rugged performance at Harlequins the previous week, they were cast-iron certainties. For their part, Quins needed something from their visit to Welford Road – no easy task on the face of it, but not impossible, given the Tigers' poor form.

As it turned out, Sale messed up badly – whatever was said in the home dressing room afterwards, it wasn't poetry – while Quins pushed Leicester every last inch of the way before falling to an opportunist try from the lightning-fast Tom Varndell, a score that raised the Midlanders from seventh (where they were out of the Heineken Cup draw as well as Premiership contention) to fourth in the blink of an eye. The champions would continue the defence of their title at Gloucester on semi-final day, with Wasps entertaining Bath.

While the latter might have won – with Lipman on the field and the best tight unit in England scrummaging strongly, they gave Wasps all the trouble they could handle – Gloucester should have won. In the event, Wasps were too good in attack for Bath, while Leicester had too much stickability for the Cherry and Whites, who looked like winners until Ryan Lamb propelled a defensive clearance vertically into the stratosphere, thereby creating the confusion that so discombobulated Iain Balshaw that he failed to distinguish between a colleague and a post. When his pass cannoned off an upright into the grateful arms of Aaron Mauger, who promptly touched down for the daftest try of this or any other season, the Tigers suddenly found themselves scenting a kill. Andy Goode's late dropped goal duly left Gloucester for dead.

And so to the final. Lawrence's day, in other words. Three years previously, it had been the day of another former England captain running down the curtain on his club career – Martin Osborne Johnson, of Leicester and the world. Wasps sensed a sentimental weakness in the Tigers that day and proceeded to smear them all over Twickenham, winning a third consecutive title in the process. Would the same boot fit the other foot? Dallaglio decreed that it should not and would not, and he was true to his word as Wasps prevailed 26-16.

Wasps, utterly focused, were far too good for Leicester in the first half; indeed, theirs was a performance fit for a crowd of almost 82,000 – the largest audience to watch a club match anywhere in the world. Haskell and Rees, in particular, brought the house down, while the celebrated skipper did his inimitable thing at close quarters. To their credit, the Tigers regrouped after suffering 40 minutes of unbridled humiliation, and they might even have gone close to pinching the spoils but for their opponents' move to uncontested scrums in the final quarter.

This was the one note of dissonance in the great symphony of the final – a final almost good enough to persuade those traditionalists who crave a return to the first-past-the-post league system that the play-off arrangements are the way forward. Marcelo Loffreda, the Argentinian who coached the Pumas to a podium finish at the World Cup before taking over at Welford Road, certainly felt betrayed. 'The rules on this must change,' he said afterwards. 'For us, it caused not only a technical problem, but a problem of psychology. The scrum was part of the virtuous circle we were trying to create for ourselves, the key to staying on the front foot and applying pressure. When I saw what was happening, I said to myself: "What is this?" I was frustrated. Deeply frustrated.'

Loffreda would soon have all the time he needed to ponder the injustices of IRB regulations on scrum safety, for within days he had been sacked. It was a painful moment – a harsh judgment on an honourable man who had barely had time to memorise the names of his players – and it put the argument over uncontested scrums in its proper perspective.

Farewell the Warrior
What Now for Lawrence Dallaglio?

by CHRIS JONES

'In typical style, he not only kept playing for Wasps after a long and painful rehabilitation but fought his way back into the England team and was part of the World Cup defence'

Lawrence Dallaglio riding off into the rugby sunset – are you mad? The London Wasps and England icon may have quit playing the sport he loves, but he will be coming to a television screen or rugby pitch near you next season.

Rugby makes Dallaglio tick and even though he will now be referred to as 'former this' and 'former that' his relevance to the game remains unquestioned. Dallaglio has been asked to help choose the back-row forwards for the 2009 Lions tour to South Africa and will also be coaching the

Richmond forwards when his old Wasps team-mate Buster White needs to freshen up the sessions. Then there are the various business ventures. He has set up The Green Room hospitality business, which offers corporate entertainment packages at all of England's home games, and purchased The Havelock pub, voted the third-best gastro pub in London by Harden's Gastro Pub Ratings.

Dallaglio also has an important role as associate director of Wasps that will see him concentrate on boosting sponsorship income and complete the search for a new stadium near High Wycombe. It's a packed diary and one that must also accommodate television punditry.

Dallaglio, whose eighty-fifth England cap came in the 2007 World Cup final defeat against South Africa, is taking his RFU Level 3 coaching exams to ensure he has all the right qualifications for that particular avenue, and many are predicting a role for him in a couple of seasons at Wasps. Dallaglio said, 'I'd be lying if I said I wouldn't like to coach at the highest level. But that's not something I expect just to walk into.

'So I'll continue to learn and talk to the right people and get whatever coaching qualifications I need while exploring other opportunities for the next two or three years. But a role I do feel I can play is off the field at Wasps. Times are changing and it's up to us to really pull together as a group off the field and demonstrate the same spirit we have on it.'

Having won the World Cup with England and the Heineken Cup twice with Wasps, who along with Leicester have dominated the domestic scene in England, Dallaglio is used to being a winner. He gave the club a standing in the sport that has not been matched by the size of the stadium at Wycombe or the number of fans who turn up for every match. Wasps need to dramatically increase their revenue after they posted another big loss despite marking Dallaglio's final season with the

Guinness Premiership title. Patently, off the pitch, Wasps need a hero – and who better than the man who filled exactly that role on it for nearly two decades?

Dallaglio has never been one to avoid verbally interacting with the opposition or the public; and blessed with a quick mind and a grasp of English polished by a period at Ampleforth College in North Yorkshire, he normally manages to have the last word. Referees were constantly offered free advice, which, over the years, elicited a heated response from opposition fans. This ability now makes him a must for television and a natural frontman for Wasps' bid for a new stadium.

There was only one occasion during his playing career when he desperately wanted to shout back at a large group of supporters but realised it would have been futile. Following the World Cup win in 2003, Dallaglio and Sir Clive Woodward – both Chelsea fans – were given the chance to do a lap of honour at Stamford Bridge at half-time during a big match. As the two waved and accepted the applause, the Chelsea fans struck up a chant. Dallaglio, over many years, had been one of those Blues fans delivering the chants from the now departed Shed and now he was discovering what it was like to be on the receiving end. He takes up the story, 'As Clive and I were going around the edge of the pitch the crowd started singing "Where were you when you were shit, where were you when you were shit?"

'I wanted to shout back "on the Shed" but realised I just had to take it!'

Of course, on most other occasions Dallaglio did get his point of view over and it served the Wasps cause well during matches. Create the right atmosphere and anything can happen. We saw that in Dublin during the semi-final victory over Munster, and again at Twickenham when Wasps defeated Toulouse to become Heineken Cup champions in 2004.

His regular confrontations with Leicester were legendary, with one of the most-used pictures in recent years showing Dallaglio being half-strangled by Martin Corry, who clearly found the comments and actions of his England sidekick unbelievably irritating. Martin Johnson, who leaned heavily on Dallaglio during the 2003 World Cup, was also wound up by the Wasps captain, and while the pair had totally different lifestyles and personalities, they were great 'rugby warriors'. Where

Johnson got in first was announcing his departure from the game. By leaving at the very zenith having lifted the Rugby World Cup, the Leicester colossus will forever live in the memory as that smiling, white-shirted leader who conquered the world. Even if he has a disaster as England's new team manager, his place in the sport is assured.

Dallaglio opted to continue playing, believing his various injuries meant there was time to make up, but a serious ankle break on the Lions tour to New Zealand in 2005 left him with a five-inch plate in his leg. In typical style, he not only kept playing for Wasps after a long and painful rehabilitation but fought his way back into the England team and was part of the World Cup defence in France in 2007. A truly heroic effort for a true rugby hero.

While Dallaglio knew he no longer had the electric pace that marked him out as a special player during England's shock Rugby World Cup Sevens triumph in Scotland in 1993, his desire for trophies remained. It was a drive that first developed at Ampleforth, where he had arrived harbouring thoughts of becoming a footballer with his beloved Chelsea. Thankfully, for Wasps and England, Ampleforth, that famous Catholic institution, made one of its most significant conversions.

A raw talent was turned into an international-class forward, and that is something the Wasps club has achieved for many years, with Tom Rees and James Haskell the latest examples to break into the Test arena. Dallaglio said, 'I was a product of our outstanding youth system and the academy at Wasps is vitally important. From the first moment young players arrive, they train and interact with the senior guys and that's a great way to learn your trade.

'It's part of the culture at Wasps to produce and foster young talent and, hopefully, those guys will also stay for 10 or 12 years to keep the traditions going. There is no better feeling that to win a game and celebrate with team-mates you have trained long and hard with for those special moments. I don't do individual sports very well.'

BELOW Dallaglio and Martin Johnson share a word after the Guinness Premiership fixture between Wasps and Leicester Tigers at The Causeway Stadium in November 2004. Might the double act one day re-form?

And that is why Lawrence Bruno Nero Dallaglio will be keeping close contact with the sport through his directorship at Wasps and commitment to help Richmond with forward coaching on an ad hoc basis. With Johnson now England team manager, who would bet against him calling on Dallaglio, his old sparring partner, to sort out future problems? They were a great double act and could be again.

Munster Turn the Tide
the 2008 Heineken Cup Final

by ALASTAIR HIGNELL

'O'Connell snatched the ball back off O'Gara … Three points would have stretched the Munster lead, but a missed penalty might have allowed Toulouse to launch a counterattack'

What's the French for *annus horribilis*? The 2007-08 season had promised so much for Les Tricolores, with France going into a World Cup on their own soil as Six Nations champions and the richest clubs in the world expected to get value for money on the European stage. Yet with Munster's Heineken Cup final defeat of Toulouse at the Millennium Stadium, it ended in *rien*. Not only did the national side fail to reach the RWC final, but moneybags teams Stade Français, Clermont Auvergne and Biarritz were also unable to reach the knockout stages of the European Cup. Toulouse alone among French clubs reached the last four, but despite entering the Cardiff showdown as slight favourites, the most decorated club in the history of the competition had to bend the knee to their only real rivals.

Munster may have lifted the trophy only once previously, compared with Toulouse's three titles; they may have been appearing in their fourth final, one fewer than their opponents; their win tally down the 13 seasons of the competition may have been slightly inferior, at 64 to 66 – but their ten consecutive seasons in the knockout stages was unrivalled, even by Toulouse.

Despite their pedigree, both teams had made heavy weather of reaching the final. Both had to fight their way out of the so-called 'pools of death', which a revamped seeding system beginning next season will

> **BELOW** Referee Nigel Owens blows for no-side and the Munster celebrations begin.

render obsolete, and both teams lost two matches in the process. Indeed, Munster had two outrageous slices of fortune against Clermont Auvergne – the try bonus point they gained when the French club sent an understrength team to Thomond Park was as instrumental as the losing bonus point the outplayed Munstermen somehow burgled in the return leg at Stade Michelin. Meanwhile, Toulouse managed to top their group despite losing away to both Leicester and Leinster, the try bonus points they earned at home against Leinster and Edinburgh earning them a home tie against Cardiff in the quarters.

Forty-one more points in front of their own fans suggested that the Toulouse juggernaut was back on track, and a Cardiff collision with Munster seemed inevitable as the Irishmen put Guinness Premiership leaders Gloucester firmly in their place at Kingsholm. But semi-finals that on paper looked easy enough for the Heineken heavyweights proved to be altogether tougher on grass. On the Saturday, injury-ravaged Toulouse suffered a Topsy Ojo-induced fright against London Irish before edging home 21-15. The next day, Munster conceded an early try to Saracens and survived a late onslaught before breathing a final-whistle sigh of relief at 18-16.

Nerves had been calmed by the time of the final. Toulouse, though still without Clément Poitrenaud and Vincent Clerc, were beginning to get their big hitters back on the field; Munster were relaxed, rested and ready to propel coach Declan Kidney into the Ireland hierarchy on a

RIGHT Doug Howlett races towards the line for what he thinks will be a Munster try. An infringement earlier in the move, though, saw the score disallowed.

BELOW Toulouse skipper Fabien Pelous gets a yellow card for a toe-poke at Alan Quinlan.

wave of emotion. The omens, they felt, were good. They had already played two Heineken finals at the Millennium Stadium and although they had lost the first to Leicester after an infamous bit of sharp practice from Tigers flanker Neil Back, they had beaten Biarritz in glorious fashion in 2006 to earn their first title from their third final appearance. What's more, they had won the toss to run out from the same north dressing room they had used that day. Toulouse may have won the other toss – they chose to play in red jerseys, leaving Munster in an unfamiliar blue – but the stadium, whose roof was to be closed despite the bright sunshine, was still bound to be a sea of Munster red and, given the fans' legendary ingenuity in acquiring tickets, to resound to 'Fields of Athenry'.

But not immediately. In fact, Toulouse started not so much like an express train as like a sleek TGV. With All Black scrum half Byron Kelleher probing away in his trademark pugnacious fashion and France No. 9 Jean-Baptiste Elissalde pulling the strings from outside half, Toulouse gave more than a glimpse of the mesmerising, multi-faceted, offloading style of play that, on their day, makes them the most feared attacking force in Europe. Yannick Jauzion, at one time acclaimed the best centre in the world before a debilitating loss of form and fitness, carved holes; Cédric Heymans menaced from full back; and Shaun Sowerby rampaged from No. 8. In the set piece, the scrum looked solid, and the line out that had taken London Irish apart in the semi-final was in ominous good order.

The first 15 minutes belonged entirely to Toulouse. Elissalde landed a dropped goal and missed a penalty, but such was the ascendancy of the men in red that it didn't seem to matter. Munster were on the back foot and scrambling for their lives, but in the midst of the mayhem at least the defence was functioning, with Rua Tipoki and Lifeimi Mafi in lumberjack mode at its heart. And when Elissalde resorted to another dropped-goal attempt, and failed, those of a Munster persuasion could begin to hope that, just maybe, the tide was beginning to turn.

Their team certainly thought so. With captain Paul O'Connell leading from the front and exuding aggression and physicality and power, the Munster pack transformed themselves from resistance fighters to overlords. A series of drives catapulted Denis Leamy over the line only for the No. 8 to lose control of the ball in the act of touching down. No matter. At the next scrum, Toulouse, unforgivably distracted by their lucky escape, coughed up the ball and this time Leamy made no mistake. Nor did Ronan O'Gara with the conversion. The outside half, another desperate to put behind him a poor World Cup and an indifferent Six Nations, then kicked his first penalty to open up a crucial seven-point lead, and his second to restore it after Elissalde had replied in kind on the stroke of half-time.

BELOW LEFT The cool boot of Ronan O'Gara kept nosing Munster ahead of the Frenchmen. The fly half finished with a tally of three penalties and the conversion of Denis Leamy's try.

BELOW O'Gara was unable to prevent Yannick Jauzion from hacking on after Cédric Heymans' audacious counterattack. Yves Donguy (behind Jauzion) would beat the cover to the ball to score for Toulouse and keep their hopes alive.

That lead was wiped out by a trademark exhibition of Toulouse brilliance. Full back Heymans, so fallible in the semi-final against London Irish, retrieved a long clearance kick inside his own half, took a quick line out to himself, chipped past the first wave of onrushing Munstermen, regathered and chipped once more as the defence closed in again. Jauzion got the first boot to the ball inside Munster's 22 and Yves Donguy won the ensuing race to touch down for a try as good as any ever seen at the Millennium Stadium.

It was even more remarkable considering Toulouse had only 14 players on the field at the time. Former France captain Fabien Pelous had been sent to the sin-bin for a half-hearted retaliatory toe-poke into the backside of Alan Quinlan after the two had squared up to each other in an off-the-ball incident. Pelous' action was not malicious; even so, it was inexcusable. It cost his team three points immediately and it condemned the remaining seven Toulouse forwards to ten minutes' hard graft at the very time that Munster were turning the screw. To make matters worse, soon after his return Pelous conceded another penalty, calmly potted by O'Gara, and that in the end proved the difference between the teams on the scoreboard as Munster went on to prevail 16-13.

On the field, the contrast was much starker. Munster finished the match in almost total control, hanging on to the ball for long periods in a series of highly skilful but crashingly dull pick-and-drives and squeezing the life out of Toulouse on the rare occasions the Frenchmen laid hands on the ball. O'Connell was at the heart of the action, repeatedly offering himself as the target man for Munster's forward drives, visibly urging discipline and single-minded rigour on his team. At one point in the

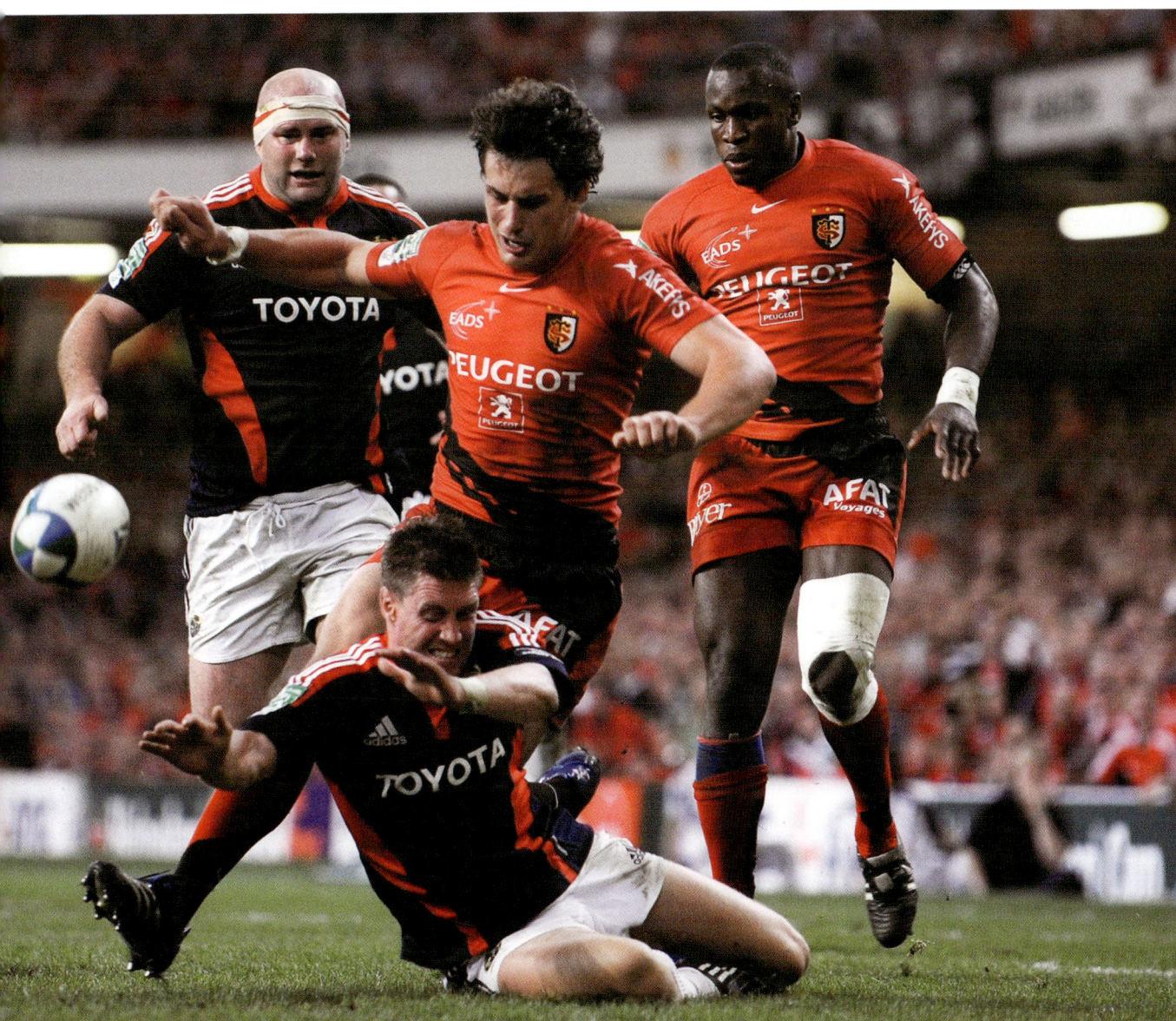

RIGHT *Alastair Hignell retired from the BBC commentary team at the end of the Guinness Premiership final but will continue to write for the Wooden Spoon Rugby World as he has done for the past 13 years. Before turning to broadcasting, Alastair won 14 caps for England at rugby and played first-class cricket for Gloucestershire. At a recent dinner in London the whole of the England 1980 Grand Slam team turned out to lend their support in raising funds for Alastair's continuing battle against MS.*

final few minutes, O'Connell snatched the ball back off O'Gara when a penalty was awarded. Three points would have stretched the Munster lead, but a missed penalty might have allowed Toulouse to launch a counterattack. O'Connell demanded the kick to touch, and Toulouse stayed in the straitjacket.

Munster's fans, as expected, partied long into the night. If anything, this victory was even sweeter than the one they had enjoyed at the same stadium two years previously. The win over Biarritz had got the monkey off their backs; after years of near misses, and two heartbreaking final defeats, they had proved – to themselves as much as anyone else – that they had what it took to become champions. But this win showed something else. Even though the likes of O'Gara, O'Connell and the remarkable John Hayes remained, the team had evolved with the times, and so had their style of play. Even though victory in the final demanded bucketloads of true and traditional Munster grit, the emergence of youngsters Tomas O'Leary and Denis Hurley and the arrival of All Black record try scorer Doug Howlett suggested that Munster had mastered more than one way of winning. Having got to the top, Munster had found a way of staying there. And even though Declan Kidney has taken over the reins at Ireland, and even though Jim Williams has returned to Australia, there's every indication that Munster will never surprise anyone in Europe again.

The benchmark has been set, the challenge has been made, Munster have taken Toulouse's mantle. By dint of pedigree, cash and playing strength, the Frenchmen have started every Heineken Cup campaign so far as favourites. Not next year. The team to fear is Munster.

> **LEFT** With the Heineken Cup on its way back to the Munster trophy cabinet, departing coach Declan Kidney leads the celebrations at the Millennium Stadium.

The Return of Bath
the 2008 Challenge Cup Final

by TERRY COOPER

'Bath's success ended a ten-year trophyless gap since they became the first English side to win the Heineken Cup. That decade included four losing finals'

Steve Borthwick and Olly Barkley were hard-bitten, influential figures in constructing Bath's win over Worcester in the European Challenge Cup final – and then emotions overwhelmed them. Both had played their last match for the club, and captain Borthwick's face was an amazing mix of regretful tears and a winner's delighted smiles. Borthwick is now a Saracen, as well as an England touring captain, while Barkley has moved to Gloucester and had just enjoyed a sample of a packed Kingsholm, his new home. Meanwhile, England's near monopoly of this second-tier – but not second-quality – event had been restored after Clermont's triumph in 2007. English teams have taken the trophy seven times in eight seasons. Winning means a berth in the following season's lucrative Heineken Cup, qualification for which is not an issue for the Irish, Scottish or Welsh teams, who hardly have to get out of bed to appear in it. Among Bath's support were Harlequins, who

entered the Heineken Cup by the back door because Bath became doubly qualified.

Bath's success ended a ten-year trophyless gap since they became the first English side to win the Heineken Cup. That decade included four losing finals, as well as topping the Premiership in 2004 just when that distinction mysteriously became an unrecognised feat, an irrelevance, because of the play-offs. Bath coach Steve Meehan said, 'The players gave everything. It removes all those questions of not winning anything for ten years. We were very disappointed to lose the Premiership semi-final against Wasps. During this match we made errors. We played a tighter game because of the conditions, although we did throw the ball around to set up the second try. We were the better team whatever some may have made of some of the refereeing calls.

'I hope we can build on this for next season because this should be the start of something. You can't stand still.'

Borthwick had given a king-sized hint after losing the 2007 final that he would be on his way, comparing the management's lack of ambition unfavourably with the players' vision. Twelve months on, he said, 'The end of the season is when you are judged. It has been a mammoth effort. For some of us the season started by preparing for the World Cup in France and for the others it began by running up and down mountains in Wales. I'm looking forward to what's ahead of me, but this weekend I will be enjoying and recalling the time I've had with these boys. It's been an honour and privilege to have played alongside so many great players at Bath over the years.'

Barkley commented, 'The way we've played this season showed that the belief is there and this side, even without me and Steve, will go on to bigger things.

'Today was not about rugby for me, it was about leaving a group of people that I love. I will keep in touch with these boys and I will miss them dearly.'

Meanwhile, Danny Grewcock reflected, 'We've had some disappointments in finals over the last few seasons, but this was a big day for the club with guys transferring or retiring. Losing out in the semi-finals of the Premiership was a blow, but that meant we had to make the most of this last chance.'

Bath had emerged from a pool containing Albi, Overmach Rugby Parma and Auch to beat Leeds 57-5 in the quarter-finals and Sale 36-14 in the semis. Worcester's pool opposition had been Bucharest, Montauban and Gran Parma, while in the knockout stages they overcame Montpellier 36-26 and Newcastle 31-16 to line up against Bath in what turned out to be an aggressive street fight of a final played in rain and a fierce wind. The Premiership is a hard man's tournament, but this match seemed on a higher level of violent contact. The hits – legal and illegal – were ferocious throughout and confrontations frequent. There was passionate, pumped-up intensity. In the opening seconds, Bath full back Nick Abendanon was clubbed by a swinging arm and tottered around like a stage drunk. It made his later try all the more creditable.

Barkley hooked an early penalty from 46 yards but was on target from similar range in the 16th minute as Worcester's technical offences were picked up by the referee. Shane Drahm soon levelled, but Worcester's chances of exerting some authority eroded when Grewcock distinguished himself with a try-saving tackle on Dale Rasmussen and played his part in Bath's burgling four first-half line-out throws. Bath hinted that it was their day with good fortune attached to the seven points they banked in the 31st minute. The try was developed down a narrow corridor near the touch line. Matt Banahan worked with Lee Mears, whose pass to Butch James was forward – but allowed. James fed Jonny Faamatuainu. Then Barkley converted off the far post. At least when Barkley struck a post with his next penalty attempt it stayed out.

Five minutes after the first try, Bath achieved a stranglehold with a second. The forwards delivered the ball right on time. James and Barkley spun it wide and Joe Maddock showed supreme dexterity and strength by slipping an underarm inside pass, while being tackled, to Abendanon. Battling Warriors kept in touch at 15-9 with two penalties from Drahm spanning the interval.

Bath's kickers closed out the result with three strikes between the 54th and 77th minutes. Barkley added a 50-yard penalty and a dropped goal from 40 yards, while James collected a penalty. Nevertheless, Worcester signed off defiantly with a last-move try, Netani Talei making an outside break for Thinus Delport to sprint in at the corner. Joe Carlisle converted – 24-16.

Worcester's appearance in the final was another symbol of how far owner Cecil Duckworth's project had come since 1995, when the club were operating seven levels below the Premiership. Never mind the glittering prizes of Leicester and Wasps, these promotions earned by Worcester are among the most remarkable achievements in the English professional era.

During the game, Worcester captain Pat Sanderson ear-bashed French referee Christophe Berdos frequently, notably when pleading for Grewcock and Mears to be sent to the cooler. Worcester later used euphemistic rugby-speak to criticise the referee and touch judges. They had a point. Berdos' reason for not handing Grewcock an early yellow card was 'It's a first offence.' So that's all right, then. You can do what you like – once. Then a touch judge could not identify Mears, who perpetrated a try-ruining late tackle. 'I did not see his number,' though the incident took place two yards from him. Sanderson said, 'We might have had a better rub of the green. We have to learn to manage referees better. But we take nothing away from Bath. We came up short. But Worcester is still an exciting place to be.'

For his part, Worcester coach Mike Ruddock observed, 'I am satisfied with my first season here. We will be better for this cup run. We had a bad start to the season, but in the last four months we won regularly. Perhaps it takes losing in a final to make you more streetwise next time.'

BELOW Skipper Steve Borthwick, on his way to Saracens, lifts Bath's first trophy in ten years.

South Africa Rugby Legends

Every great idea or vision starts off as a seed that, with time and nurturing, grows into a beautiful flower. The Legends concept is one of th visions.

Developing the great game of rugby, since 2002 the South African Rugby Legends Association (SARLA) is a charitable trust organisation base South Africa.

SARLA was founded by John Allan, former Springbok, Scottish and Sharks hooker, and long time friend Gavin Varejes, together with a group their contemporaries. The core focus of SARLA is to build up the game of rugby at grass-roots and club rugby level. SARLA, made up of form Springbok and provincial players, provides a vehicle for the ex-players to put something back into "their" game through the social responsibilit programmes.

The South African Rugby Legends Association has four social responsibilities:

IQHAWE

Iqhawe - translated "Hero" or "Champion" in Xhoza- is a project run by the eLan Rugby Legends to raise the bar on rugby evelopment throughout South Africa.

The project is co-ordinated countrywide with the respective provincial unions. 4,500 children take part in a talent identificati tournament. 40 top players are selected to attend lectures and development programmes for eight months, the aim being that by the end of programme the players will be upstanding members of their communities.

STREET KIDS CRIME PREVENTION

In Street Kids Crime Prevention programme, eLan Rugby Legends along with the South African Police Services strategic team are planning address the ever-present issue of children living on the streets.

SARLA will work with the Police Commissioners from each division utilising their logistics and network to get kids off the street and playi sport. Daily programmes will be held with various sporting bodies and in the evenings the children will be housed in confiscated buildings. T target is to reunite the children with their families and their communities.

ADOPT A SCHOOL

Legends are addressing the need to transform and develop not only rugby but also broader education needs at a grass-roots level by creating their Adopt-A-School programme.

SARLA has approached the top 100 playing rugby schools which will in turn adopt four schools in the disadvantaged areas in their vicinity and provide them with school books and equipment and include them in their sports days.

LEAVING A LEGACY

The biggest individual sports event, the 2010 World Cup Soccer that will take place in South Africa, is the catalyst for Leaving a Legacy, the newe programme that the Legends have undertaken. The programme goes into specified areas where land is developed. A synthetic surface,Tigerturf laid and a community / club house facility built next to it. These Legacy Parks can be used by the community for sporting events or gatherings.

The eLan / SARLA **'FIELD OF DREAMS'** initiative aims to raise funds for SARLA's social development programmes. The eLan Group hav generously donated a plot of land at the Blythedale Coastal Resort which will be raffled off once four thousand pledges have been made ar honoured.

The 'Field of Dreams' initiative is an international competition with former players as ambassadors. Five countries have been selected and eac ambassador will select the charity of their choice in their country. All money raised will be split between the selected charity and SARLA's soci development programme.

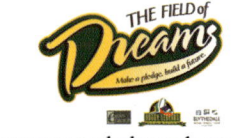

www.sarugbylegends.co.za

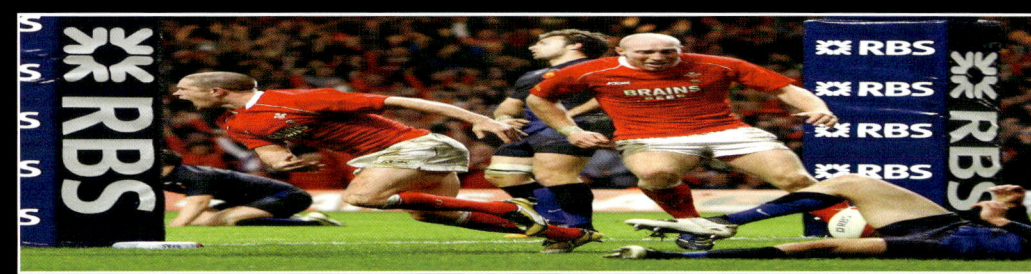

REVIEW OF THE
SEASON 2007-08

Grand Slam Gatland the 2008 Six Nations Championship

by CHRIS JONES

'Wales, on the other hand, with wonder wing Shane Williams at his brilliant best, were having a season to savour and confirmed their attacking prowess and defensive solidity'

The RBS Six Nations Championship produced a Grand Slam for Wales and extra revenue for the Severn Bridge toll booths. A ground-breaking 'job share' saw Wasps head coach Shaun Edwards team up again with his close friend and former Wasps director of rugby Warren Gatland, who was appointed the Wales head coach going into the championship. It meant Edwards spent hours travelling up and down the M4 and had to pay the toll every time he entered Wales!

The choice of coaching staff was a marvellously forward-thinking move by the Welsh Rugby Union – not a phrase normally associated with the WRU – and they gave Gatland and Edwards an even better chance of success by signing up Rob Howley from Cardiff Blues, who as a scrum half had enjoyed Heineken Cup triumph at Wasps with those two brilliant coaches.

Suddenly the Welsh squad had one of the most impressive coaching units in world rugby on board, and how English fans were envious. Edwards should have been undertaking the same

defensive role with England, but where the WRU were more than happy to break new ground with a job share involving Wasps, the RFU claimed their own rules made this a non-starter. It was a pitiful performance from the RFU hierarchy and is going to remove Edwards from their orbit until after RWC 2011 in New Zealand.

Instead of giving Brian Ashton the skills of Edwards to supplement the runners-up place achieved at the World Cup in France, England left their head coach to run exactly the same misfiring coaching panel, which managed second place in the Six Nations before Ashton was dumped with the arrival of Martin Johnson. The handling of the whole affair – post-World Cup – left a nasty taste in many mouths, and only Ashton would emerge with any credit.

The coaching issue – revolving around Edwards – made the opening day of the championship even more relevant as England hosted Wales at Twickenham. Everything was going Ashton's way until an inexplicable collapse in the second half, when experienced players

such as Jonny Wilkinson and Mike Tindall lost their heads, undermined the performance. Suddenly it was Wales in the ascendant, and there was Edwards – a proud Englishman – bounding down the West Stand steps, yelling instructions to his backs to drop deep and not give England anything in the final ten minutes.

The scoreboard showed England 19 Wales 26 and the ramifications of that result would only really be seen after the championship was over. The Twickenham match helped erase the opening weekend's other two games from the memory. Ireland came desperately close to an embarrassing home defeat by Italy, who were under the control, for the first time, of new coach Nick Mallett – another England could have signed but let get away! Ireland hung on to take the match 16-11, and pressure was immediately on head coach Eddie O'Sullivan, who would eventually pay the ultimate price for failing to get the trophies this golden generation of Irish players was good enough to collect at Test level. France, meanwhile, won away at Murrayfield as Scotland were hammered 27-6 and another long unhappy championship looked set to unfold for the Scots under coach Frank Hadden.

ABOVE England's new playmaker Danny Cipriani escapes the clutches of Shane Horgan in England's 33-10 win over Ireland at Headquarters.

Every single head coach would be put under the spotlight during this campaign, and while Ashton and O'Sullivan would be binned, Mallett, Gatland, Hadden and Marc Lièvremont, the new French supremo, would survive. Former France back-rower Lièvremont would operate a revolving-door selection policy which went some way to helping Wales win the Grand Slam and elevating England to second place. He kept his job, but that cavalier attitude will not be tolerated by the French rugby public next season.

France and Wales each remained unbeaten after two games played, the French having defeated Ireland 26-21 second up, with a hat-trick from Vincent Clerc, their outstanding wing. For their part, the Welsh turned the Millennium Stadium into a cauldron of joy, beating Scotland 30-15. The Scots were truly average and the portents were not good for Hadden. On the Sunday, Ashton saw his England team struggle to hand Italy a 23-19 defeat in Rome.

Despite their stuttering start, England, as they did in the World Cup semi-final, found their form against the French and won 24-13 at Stade de France to open up the championship race and leave English fans wondering, first, just how good were their heroes, and, second, should they play all their matches against Les Bleus in Paris? The pressure on Ashton was transferred to Lièvremont, although it was hard to tell as he kept on making fundamental changes to personnel. Meanwhile, the England team and Jonny Wilkinson's place in the great scheme of things was the most pressing talking point. Wales, on the other hand, with wonder wing Shane Williams at his brilliant best, were having a season to savour and confirmed their attacking prowess and defensive solidity under Gatland, Edwards and Howley by destroying Italy 47-8, while the Irish appeared to push Hadden even closer to the sack by winning 34-13 at Croke Park. The Irish took great heart from this result, and O'Sullivan seemed safer than his Scotland counterpart – how wrong we were.

On the fourth Sunday, France got their show back on the road with more changes and a hard-fought 25-13 win over Italy in Paris. The day before, Wales had arrived at Croke Park in search of Triple Crown glory. A fantastic match seesawed all over the place before Gatland's men emerged victorious 16-12, and with the Grand Slam in sight. At Murrayfield, Scotland were supposed to fall over and meekly accept defeat at home to England, but once again the heavens opened on the English and they were found wanting. England's cause was not helped by a midweek, mid-night visit to a London nightclub by Wasps wonderkid Danny Cipriani, who was due to make his first England start against the Scots. He was dropped and warned about future conduct – and it proved to be a good match to miss. It was 'Groundhog Day' for so many of the England old hands as they trooped off the pitch in sodden kit having lost to a Scotland team no one feared. The scoreboard showed the Scots had won 15-9, and that man Hadden was able to look his critics in the eye and utter a loud but hollow 'told you so' message.

Scotland had to travel to Rome on the final weekend, and the locals scrapped it out with the visitors for a 23-20 win, courtesy of a late dropped goal. Even so, because of points difference, the Italians still ended up with the Wooden Spoon – although the way that coach Mallett and his men celebrated at the final whistle showed that all that really mattered was getting the 'W'. For Hadden, the result somehow kept him his job!

England, with Danny Cipriani at outside half, produced a wonderful finale at Twickenham for their long-suffering fans, and put the final nail in O'Sullivan's coffin at the same time, with a 33-10 win. It was an indication of what Cipriani could do for England. Now we have to wait and hope that his dreadful ankle break does not keep him out for too long.

All eyes then turned to Cardiff and a possible Grand Slam in front of 80,000 fans who were up for a big party. Wales had to subdue a French side that started to show glimpses of what would be possible if their head coach ever settled on a favourite XV and were good value for a 29-12 win that launched celebrations in the Principality that lasted for days. Gatland and Edwards and the rest of their coaching team had worked a minor miracle, with the help of Martyn Williams' play at No. 7, captain Ryan Jones's leadership and, most of all, six-try Shane Williams, who had produced all kinds of heroics during the championship. For once, twinkling feet had overcome brute force – and how a nation and the sport itself rejoiced.

BELOW Shane Williams becomes Wales's all-time top Test try scorer with 41 as the Grand Slam inches ever closer against France in Cardiff.

The Club Scene
England: An Up-and-Down Year
by BILL MITCHELL

'Gloucester finished top of the Guinness Premiership table, but once again we had the absurd situation of the club with the best record … leaving the season with nothing'

As the excellence – or otherwise – of any international team is usually measured by its performances in major competitions, England's can be judged accordingly. It will be a little bit misleading, since the team reached the final of the Rugby World Cup in France and was second to Wales in the Six Nations, with the overall record in competitive matches since this same period last year possibly showing an improvement.

There were some excellent efforts and some that were less distinguished, while the overall record was played fourteen, won eight and lost six, which amounts to pass marks that were badly marred by a visit to New Zealand and two heavy defeats (37-20 and 44-12).

ABOVE Try scorer Mathew Tait waltzes past David Croft during the England XV v Barbarians match at Twickenham, won 17-14 by the hosts.

FACING PAGE John Ireland's caricature of England and Wasps winger Paul Sackey.

England's best player discoveries were the two wings of West African origin – Topsy Ojo (whose family is from Nigeria and who scored two tries against New Zealand) and Paul Sackey (whose parents are from Ghana).

In the Rugby World Cup, England finished in second place in Pool A with victories over Samoa, the United States and Tonga offset by an horrific 36-0 thrashing by eventual champions South Africa. This result brought about (or so it was alleged) something of a palace revolution and a transformation to the extent that Australia lost in the quarter-finals to a superb England forward effort spearheaded by prop Andrew Sheridan. Then, in the semis, France, caught napping by an early England try, were also eliminated. They had rediscovered their form but then paid the penalty for caution by conceding some late points to the not always so reliable boot of Jonny Wilkinson, who might well have been awarded a knighthood had his form in the final been better than it was. Wilkinson always gave everything in terms of tackling – almost suicidally – but he has probably lost something where pace is needed and his tactical kicking has been better.

Even so, England approached the Stade de France final in upbeat mood, but apart from a narrow miss in terms of a try thanks to a marvellous run by Mathew Tait, Mark Cueto's foot just hitting the touch line in his dive to touch down, the side rarely threatened a superior Springbok outfit, which eventually was not flattered by the 15-6 scoreline. The points all came from kicks, but the winners could well have been awarded at least one penalty try in the first half and the line-out dominance of the massive Victor Matfield was just too much; attempts to disturb Percy Montgomery with long-range punts also failed.

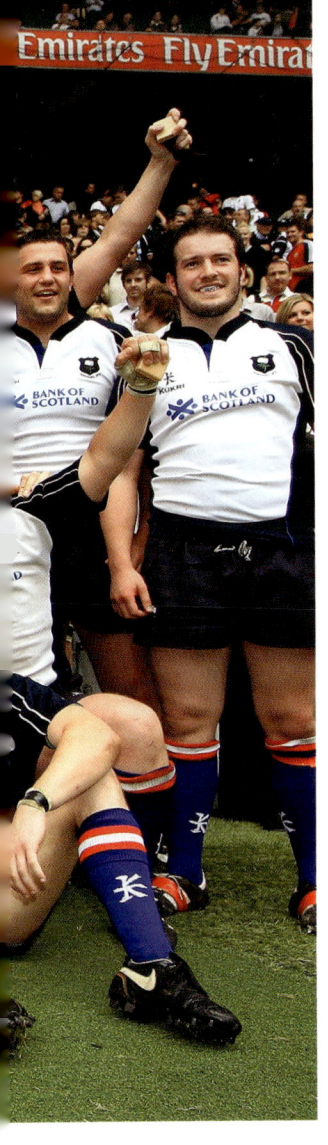

The Six Nations campaign could not have got off to a worse start, with a comfortable winning position against Wales at Twickenham being transformed into a 19-26 defeat. The visit to Rome almost brought a repeat story, but the side held out against strong late pressure, while the trip to Paris brought an altogether better performance, with another great forward effort bringing with it a superb victory.

So there was every reason to believe that Murrayfield should produce success, but a dire match in poor conditions meant that the Calcutta Cup was left behind in Scotland, who well deserved a 15-9 win, with all their points coming from the ever-dependable boot of Chris Paterson. England's talisman Wilkinson, on the other hand, suffered the indignity of being substituted and then replaced for the final match of the campaign against Ireland by Danny Cipriani, who was a star in a comprehensive triumph. But the new fly half was to suffer a very bad ankle injury in a club semi-final later in the season and his future must be in doubt. We wish him all the very best, since men of his talent are in short supply.

Another tour from hell followed in New Zealand, with heavy defeats accompanied by a sad lack of discipline off the park – all after Martin Johnson had been announced as the new manager of the team. Everyone will wish him well while not envying his task.

All was not doom and gloom in the country, however, as the Under 20 team did a Grand Slam of their own and also reached the final of the inaugural IRB Junior World Championship in Wales, where only New Zealand (who else?) were better. The Churchill Cup, contested in North

LEFT Yorkshire skipper Dan Cook and his troops and support celebrate with the Bill Beaumont Cup after beating Devon 33-13 in the final of the County Championship at Twickenham.

BELOW Man of the Match Dave Blyth of Birkenhead Park crashes over for one of his two tries in the final of the EDF Energy Intermediate Trophy, eventually won by Chester, 21-18, after wing Matt Sheen ran in the crucial score from 90 yards in the 73rd minute.

America, saw the England Saxons retain the trophy against a brave Scottish team in the final, while the Sevens outfit continues to be probably Europe's best, with a match victory over New Zealand a fine achievement; even so, the southern hemisphere sides are generally too good at this version of the game.

On the club scene Gloucester finished top of the Guinness Premiership table, but once again we had the absurd situation of the club with the best record after doing all the 'hard yards' leaving the season with nothing. Gloucester went down to Leicester at home in the semis, leaving the Tigers to take on Wasps in the title decider at Headquarters, where the Londoners won 26-16. The next day, Twickenham saw Yorkshire beat Devon by a resounding 33-13 in the County Championship final as well as a feisty game between an England XV and the Barbarians, which ended 17-14 to the hosts. Since Leicester had earlier lost the EDF Energy Cup final 6-23 to the Ospreys at Twickenham, it was not to be their season. Bath, meanwhile, won the European Challenge Cup in an all-English final, beating Worcester Warriors 24-16 at Kingsholm.

To round off matters, it can be recorded that Northampton won the EDF National Trophy final, overcoming Exeter's brave effort to prevail 24-13, and Chester won a local derby against Birkenhead Park 21-18 to become EDF Intermediate champions. The Army were again the Services winners, 22-11 against the gallant men of the Royal Navy, while Hartpury College took the BUSA title and appear to be upstaging the normal top dogs, Loughborough.

Cambridge, with an excellent pack, won a good University Match against Oxford at Twickenham 22-16. It is good to see that the match still attracts decent crowds, although only optimists will claim that the switch from the traditional Tuesday afternoon to Thursday evening was a success. The clash produced one controversial incident, when the Oxford captain was the victim of a bad late tackle with just a few minutes remaining. The offence was only penalised on the intervention of the touch judge and with the award of a kick, when many thought that a yellow card should also have been flourished. I have to admit to the feeling that I think spear tackles and the late efforts, which are potentially lethal, should attract an automatic sin-binning unless the circumstances justify leniency.

The new campaign must be viewed with some trepidation by those with the best interests of England at heart, and there will be many hopes that the professional clubs try to subordinate their own selfish needs to those of the national scene, but don't hold your respective breaths. Too many politicians have their own agendas.

Scotland: Robinson's Revolution

by ALAN LORIMER

'In the event, Edinburgh got agonisingly close to pulling off what would have been a major upset by coming within a score of overcoming Toulouse at Murrayfield'

Whatever else marked out the 2007-08 Scottish professional club scene, it was the arrival north of the border of former England coach Andy Robinson that had the greatest impact. Robinson, sacked by his RFU bosses in the wake of England's 2006 autumn international series, accepted the offer to become head coach at Edinburgh, in a move that was to revive both his career and his reputation.

Edinburgh at the time of Robinson's appointment were recovering from a damaging and very public row over finances between former owner Bob Carruthers and the SRU chief executive, Gordon McKie. The deteriorating situation at the end of the previous season had contributed to a haemorrhage of senior players, among them Chris Paterson, Simon Taylor and Scott Murray, which left the club looking short of experience and with an uncertainty as to how they would survive in the Magners League and Heineken Cup.

BELOW Edinburgh flanker Roland Reid charges the Leicester pack, as Andy Robinson's side beat the Tigers 17-12 at Murrayfield in the Heineken Cup.

Robinson's first major challenge was indeed the Heineken Cup, in which Edinburgh had been drawn in the same pool as Toulouse, Leicester and Leinster. In the event, Edinburgh got agonisingly close to pulling off what would have been a major upset by coming within a score of overcoming Toulouse at Murrayfield. It was proof that Robinson was turning Edinburgh around, and confirmation came when the capital side inflicted a 29-10 defeat on Leinster before ending Leicester's qualifying hopes with a 17-12 home victory. Neither of these two wins was enough to prevent Edinburgh finishing fourth in their pool, but the level of performance was sufficiently encouraging to suggest that Robinson had instilled new thinking into his squad. Many of the young Edinburgh players, such as flanker Ross Rennie and centres Ben Cairns and Nick De Luca, are full of admiration for Robinson and appreciate in particular his ability to coach on an individual basis.

The Robinson influence was also evident in Edinburgh's Magners League results, the club finishing fourth in the table and losing only two matches in their post-Christmas programme. The only worry for the Edinburgh players is that Robinson's success might lead to promotion within Scottish rugby – many fans have already called for the former England coach to replace Frank Hadden.

Robinson's achievement has not only been in results but also in improving a number of less well-known players, among them flanker Alan MacDonald, centre/wing John Houston and scrum half Greig Laidlaw. Moreover, he has repaired the shattered confidence of stand-off Phil Godman, whose style of play fits in with the dynamic game that Robinson wants for his side.

There has, too, been improvement at Scotland's other professional club, Glasgow Warriors. Under the coaching of Sean Lineen, Glasgow finished just one place behind Edinburgh in the Magners League, and in the Heineken Cup posted enough good performances to wipe out the memory of miserable campaigns in previous years. Two wins over Viadana and a home victory against Biarritz plus two very close games with Saracens added to Glasgow's improved showing in the Heineken Cup, while in the Magners League a late charge produced five wins in the last five games. Glasgow's top player was stand-off Dan Parks, whose performances at club level contrast markedly with his much-criticised displays on the international stage. If Parks pulled the strings at Glasgow, then in the last few games it was the speed of Thom and Max Evans that provided the finishing, the brothers' scorching pace being crucial to the Warriors' try-scoring ability.

Former All Black Daryl Gibson, very much a player-coach nowadays, was also hugely influential, but arguably it was Glasgow's all-international back row of Kelly Brown, Johnnie Beattie and John Barclay who were the stand-out players. Lineen's find of the season was undoubtedly prop Moray Low, who looks certain to become a fixture in the Scotland front row.

RIGHT Glasgow's season stand-out player Dan Parks lines up a penalty in the 9-6 home Heineken Cup win over Biarritz.

FACING PAGE Andy Robinson after his Edinburgh side's 29-10 home defeat of Leinster in the Heineken Cup.

BELOW Runaway Premiership winners Boroughmuir lifted the title as early as 19 January.

While the relative success of Edinburgh and Glasgow might, in some eyes, vindicate the decision to cull the Borders professional team, the fact remains that the reduction from three to two has left Scotland with too small a base of professional players. If a third professional team is not to be re-established, and it seems unlikely in the current climate, then perhaps it is time to look at making the top end of the amateur game semi-professional. The justification for taking such a route lies in what some observers see as a rise in standards in the top layer of the Premiership, brought about by better coaching, fitter and more skilful players and the return to the amateur game of former professionals. A case in point is Boroughmuir, for whom ex-Borders professional Calum Cusiter, the older brother of Scotland scrum half Chris, was a key player in the Meggetland side's domination of the Premiership last season.

Boroughmuir made a sprint start and never slackened the pace as they established a huge lead that duly brought them the Premiership title. Besides Cusiter, Boroughmuir had experience throughout their team in players like flanker Angus Martyn, No. 8 Ben Fisher and centre Malcolm Clapperton. Then when Charlie Keenan returned from a professional stint in Spain, Boroughmuir, coached by former Scotland back-row Stuart Reid and Welshman Eamon John, gained extra pace on the wing to complement that of skipper Rory Couper.

Scottish Hydro Electric
Premiership Winners

SCOTTISH CLUB RUGBY

Brewed longer for a distinctive, full flavour

Real character doesn t happen overnight.
Nor are hidden depths immediately obvious.
But given time, they emerge.

WHEN YOU RE READY, YOU LL FIND IT.

Boroughmuir's nearest challengers were Watsonians, for whom centre Andrew Skeen, a former Newcastle Falcons Academy player, emerged as a star. But the Myreside men were adrift by 21 points at the end of the competition, underlining the huge gap between winners and runners-up.

Elsewhere, Ayr and Heriot's looked to be in the frame earlier in the season, but both clubs showed inconsistency and their challenges fell away. In the lower half of the league, relegation became an issue affecting six clubs. Dundee HSFP were the first to fall through the trap door, despite some excellent, but ultimately losing, performances in the season. Their exit from the top tier means that there is now no first division side north of the central belt. It also left a scrap to avoid the second relegation slot. In a tight finish, Hawick, Glasgow Hawks, Stirling County and Edinburgh Academicals all sweated it out, but in the end it was GHA who returned to the second division.

As one Glasgow club went down, so another, West of Scotland, was promoted to the Premiership elite. The other club to win promotion was Selkirk, which means that the 2008-09 Premiership first division will contain three Border clubs. The other good news for the Borders is that both Gala and Peebles were elevated from division three of the Premiership, confirming the impression that there has been a revival of rugby in the south of Scotland despite the loss of the professional team.

In the Scottish Hydro Electric Cup, it was Melrose who triumphed, with a 31-24 win over Heriot's in the final at Murrayfield. Melrose had looked likely winners after recovering from a mid-season slump that had killed off their chances of winning the league. Like Boroughmuir, Melrose are a side that have been together for a few years, despite the fact that they are still relatively young. But it was the arrival of former Australia Sevens player Jordan Macey that really tipped the balance between good and best. Macey's incredible speed, deployed cleverly at full back, made the difference as Melrose came through the later rounds against Glasgow Hawks, Boroughmuir and Hawick to book their place in the final.

Heriot's, too, had shown winning form late in the season – enough, certainly, to secure a place in the Murrayfield showpiece game. But on the day, Melrose dominated the first half with strong forward play and subtle touches from their pacy backs under the generalship of their up-and-coming stand-off, Scott Wight, to establish a 28-0 half-time lead.

The Goldenacre men hit back in the second half, scoring four tries, but in the end they were chasing too big a lead, leaving Melrose worthy cup winners. For their coach, former Scotland stand-off Craig Chalmers, part of the Greenyards winning team in 1997, it was a particularly pleasing denouement to a great season.

BELOW Melrose wing Callum Anderson goes over in the corner in his side's 31-24 defeat of Heriot's in the Scottish Hydro Electric Cup final at Murrayfield.

Wales: EDF Not Enough for Ospreys
by DAVID STEWART

'In winning the EDF Energy Cup [the Ospreys] enjoyed the most successful campaign of the four Welsh regions; then they parted company with their coach'

The Ospreys (the Neath-Swansea prefix has been dropped) had the best stadium, the most money, the strongest squad, and in winning the EDF Energy Cup they enjoyed the most successful campaign of the four Welsh regions; then they parted company with their coach. Beating Leicester 23-6 at Twickenham in the final of the Anglo-Welsh competition may have marked a step-up from winning the Magners League a season earlier, but Lyn Jones soon discovered it was not enough. A first XV which contained most of the Grand Slam-winning national side fell 10-19 at the quarter-final stage of the Heineken Cup against a Saracens team it had humbled 30-3 in the EDF Energy Cup only a few weeks earlier. The Heineken is now the benchmark for the ambitious men in control of the Ospreys, and Jones was considered not to have made the best of the resources at his disposal.

And examining both the playing staff and the results graph, it must be admitted they have a point. Ospreys had the nation's captain and its outstanding forward (Ryan Jones); the player of the season (the stunning Shane Williams); four front-rowers (Duncan and Adam Jones, Huw Bennett and Richard Hibbard) and three second-rows (Ians Gough and Evans plus Alun-Wyn Jones) who started Tests under Warren Gatland; and the most exciting midfield combination (James Hook and Gavin Henson). Add the influential Kiwis Justin Marshall, Filo Tiatia and especially Marty Holah and it suggests a potent workforce.

However, a season that concluded with four losses from the last five games (with the Dragons and Connacht last up) suggested a camp that was functioning at less than full throttle. Their defence of the Magners ended in a lowly seventh-place finish, too low to suggest consistency of performance. Andrew Hore, once the Wales fitness coach, has returned from his native New Zealand in the newly created post of elite performance director. The core of the Ospreys squad is still young enough to allow a decent attempt at climbing to the top rung of European rugby over the next few seasons. After all, Munster tried and failed

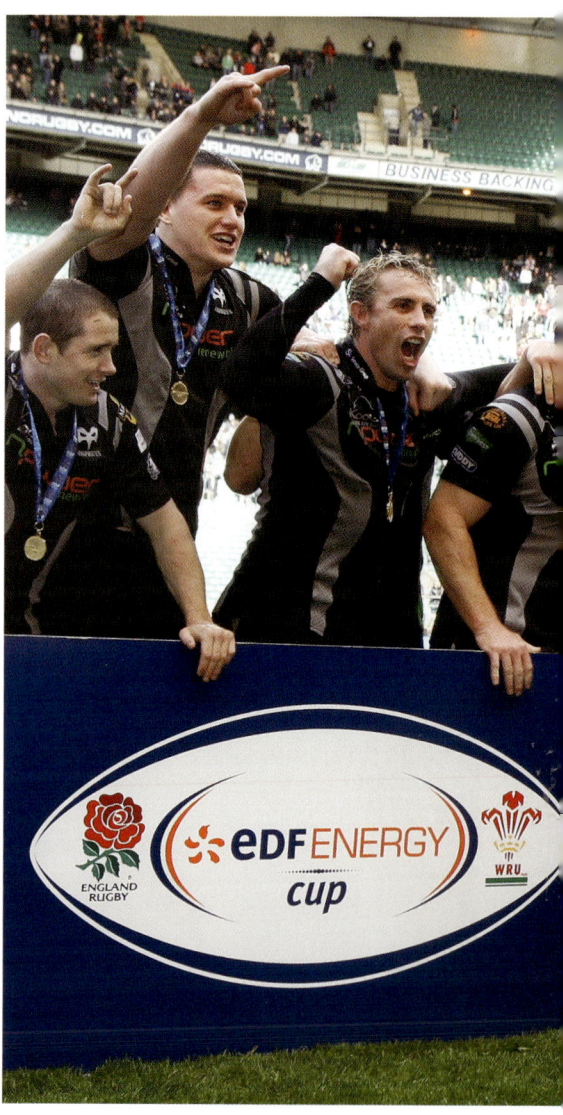

BELOW Ospreys captain Ryan Jones enjoys a shower after the EDF Energy Cup final victory over Leicester. Club coach Lyn Jones, however, was soon on his way.

twice before achieving their place at the summit. The draw for 2008-09 has the Ospreys against their old foes from Leicester once again, as well as sending them to the Catalan bear pit that is Perpignan. A tough proposition.

The Blues were the other Welsh team to get beyond the pool phases of the Heineken. In doing so, and in repeating their runners-up finish in the Magners, they may have surpassed themselves but not surprised those charged with the gradual rebuilding at the Arms Park. At the cornerstone of this has been a trio of New Zealanders – Paul Tito, Ben Blair and skipper Xavier Rush. The No. 8 has perhaps been the outstanding overseas signing of recent years. His leadership, tactical nous and ability to carry ball over the gain line have been critical to his team's progress.

That came to fruition in the two encounters with Stade Français. The Paris powerhouses were restricted to a 12-6 victory at home and vanquished 31-21 in Cardiff. Toulouse away in the quarters was predictably a step too far, but the foundations are in place for the team to compete for honours once again, a status largely denied their supporters thus far in the paid era. Several of their best-known names are likely to have a busy season ahead, with Tom Shanklin, the exceptional Martyn Williams and most of all Gethin Jenkins live contenders for Lions Test jerseys in South Africa.

The margin between the Blues and Leinster, winners of the Magners, was five points – accounted for by the Irishmen doing the double in Cardiff and Dublin. The gap to the Scarlets in sixth place

was substantial, the west Wales region forming an unflattering lower mid-table block with the Ospreys and Dragons, all finishing below the two Scottish teams. This gave rise to the distribution-of-resources debate once more. With the Borders having been wound up in 2007, and their players and funding transferred to Glasgow and Edinburgh, there was a distinct improvement in the Scots' competitiveness. Wales has already reduced its complement by one regional team, with the demise of the Celtic Warriors at the end of 2003-04. However, to formulate squads of the appropriate quality, each of the regions has recruited from overseas. The knock-on effect for the strength in depth of the Wales squad has already exercised Warren Gatland.

The Scarlets had their most unhappy spell for many years. It ended with Phil Davies being terminated in a manner which left a bad taste in the mouths of several distinguished former players. Davies' departure after two seasons at the helm opened the way for Nigel Davies as head coach and Gareth Jenkins as head of regional development and recruitment to return. Their task is hefty, as there is more than a hint of decline. For the first time, the Scarlets won not a single Heineken pool game. They finished the season with five consecutive defeats, three of them at the decrepit Stradey. Completion of the new stadium cannot come soon enough, nor the infusion of new players. The likes of Simon Easterby, Iestyn Thomas and Vernon Cooper have plenty of miles on the clock; Dwayne Peel has gone to Sale. Matthew Rees, Scott MacLeod and Morgan Stoddart of the younger generation prosper, but the future rests with the likes of Josh Turnbull (lock/back-rower), Daniel Evans (wing/full back) and Jon Davies (centre), all currently playing for Wales Under 20.

The Dragons are unfortunately the unglamorous outfit at the moment. They are under-resourced, their ground looks tired and their squad is shorn of so-called marquee names – a return of eight wins from twenty-seven competitive starts accurately reflects their status quo. Paul Turner, Dai Rees and Leigh Jones, men of Gwent all, have done well to keep the show afloat with a combination of honest pros and the odd former Welsh international like Colin Charvis and Kevin Morgan.

Their season ended with home wins over the Ospreys and Leinster (who had already secured the title), but they came after a run which produced a single draw and seven defeats. A tightening economic outlook could be bad news for an area that produced the likes of David Watkins, Keith Jarrett and Brian Price. That said, there are plans to redevelop Rodney Parade, and there have been some earthy signings from New Zealand, notably the (Waikato) Chiefs hooker Tom Willis.

Finally, the most poignant memory of the year had nothing to do with the playing side of the game. It was when decrepit old Stradey was filled for the funeral of Grav, that delightful man of rugby and much else from Mynyddygarreg, near Kidwelly. His heart and soul were in Llanelli, and that is where the grandest of goodbyes was said.

Ireland: A Topsy-Turvy Season

by SEAN DIFFLEY

'But while Munster were assuming the top spot in Europe, Leinster simply ran away with the Magners ... League. And, as many Leinster fans would say, about time too!'

It was quite a topsy-turvy season for Irish rugby. A poor Six Nations after the disappointing World Cup led to a wild outcry for the head of Eddie O'Sullivan, until then the most successful Irish team coach ever. But something was creaking, and a new contract for O'Sullivan was wafted away as he made his exit, making way for the new coach, the highly successful Declan Kidney, who had been general in charge of Munster's remarkable second Heineken Cup success. There was a fair amount of humming and hawing in the Irish rugby establishment before Kidney was prised away from Munster. As late as June, when the Irish squad travelled to New Zealand and Australia, Kidney had still not taken over, merely going Down Under in the company of new Ireland manager Paul McNaughton to view affairs from a respectful distance in the stands. Connacht's Michael Bradley was interim coach and selector as Kidney was confined to viewing the, er, landscape.

The big question agitating Irish rugby minds was whether Kidney would be capable of transferring the unique parochial ambience of Munster to the national squad. Kidney was a teacher at Presentation College, Cork, and many of the players who have manned his squad, such as Ronan O'Gara and Peter Stringer, were his pupils as small boys. Daily contact in the Munster context is a bit different to the norms of Irish squads – occasional get-togethers in Dublin is a job of a different

calibre. It will be most interesting to watch developments, and will Kidney be the recipient of all the praise and media glory if the Irish scene doesn't quite work out? Many of the present Irish squad are coming towards retirement, and although there are some very promising youngsters – Robert Kearney, Luke Fitzgerald – the situation appears very much in transition.

In the meantime, the modest Kidney can bask in the glow of having coached Munster to the championship of Europe – a quite remarkable feat. Their victory over Toulouse in the final of the Heineken Cup in Cardiff in May was awe-inspiring, a result of expert planning and execution against a side that, if allowed, would have run riot. Toulouse were the aristocrats. Three-time winners of the cup, they had played 94 Heineken matches, beating London Irish in their eighth winning semi-final to reach their fifth final.

Munster came through what some referred to as the 'pool of death', and indeed the going was tough against the reigning French champions Clermont and the redoubtable Wasps, and in the knockout stages against Gloucester and Saracens. The meeting with Saracens was Munster's seventh semi-final, but it was undoubtedly the match with Wasps at Thomond Park that clearly indicated the Irish side's basic strength. In the backs, of course, they had O'Gara, the great Kiwi wing Doug Howlett and those two centres from the South Pacific, Lifeimi Mafi and Rua Tipoki. But it was the forwards, Paul O'Connell, Donncha O'Callaghan and company, who in a downpour overcame the Wasps pack and, along with some remarkable kicking by O'Gara, ruled the day.

In the final, Munster's defence was stellar stuff, yielding just one try from a typical bit of fancy French style. In the closing stages, the Munster forwards held possession and served up a classic exhibition of pick-and-drive to win the trophy. There was a school of thought that lamented the style of play. But no fools Munster. Handing the ball to Toulouse would have been the equivalent of committing hara-kiri. Munster played to their strengths. Toulouse were unable to do so. What now for Munster? A few are over the hill, and new faces, particularly in the front row, will have to be found.

RIGHT Leo Cullen, returned from a stint at Leicester, grabs line-out ball ahead of Mick O'Driscoll in the Magners League clash at the Royal Dublin Society grounds. Leinster won 21-12 to do the double over Munster.

FACING PAGE A wet and weary-looking Denis Leamy touches down for the only try of the game, as Munster beat Wasps 19-3 at Thomond Park in round six of the Heineken Cup, sending the 2007 winners out of the competition.

But while Munster were assuming the top spot in Europe, Leinster simply ran away with the Magners, or Celtic, League. And, as many Leinster fans would say, about time too! With some excellent backs – Brian O'Driscoll, Robert Kearney, Luke Fitzgerald, Argentine captain Felipe Contepomi – Leinster had been falling short in recent seasons. But their Australian coach, Michael Cheika, had at last put a good pack in place. Springbok Ollie le Roux proved of great force and was highly popular with the fans, now accommodated in the more spacious Royal Dublin Society grounds traditionally used for equestrian events. The return from Leicester of Leo Cullen to lead the pack was also a boost for the side, and having resisted the opposition of especially Cardiff and Llanelli, Leinster took the honours.

It wasn't a very happy season for Ulster and Connacht. The latter, usually dismissed as Ireland's Cinderella province, had a couple of decent wins but still finished at the bottom of the Magners League, with a dispirited Ulster just above them. Mark McCall departed as Ulster's coach, joining Jeremy Davidson at Castres, and Matt Williams took over. David Humphreys, that talented out-half, played his last match for Ulster and the occasion of his final game at Ravenhill resulted in a prolonged ovation from a full house. And fully deserved, too. Humphreys is a solicitor by profession but has accepted a post with the Ulster Branch.

In the so-called amateur arena, the top club in Ireland again hailed from Munster – Cork Constitution. They won the All Ireland League, beating holders Garryowen 18-8 in the final. With all the emphasis on the professional game, the club sides in the All Ireland League feel neglected. They argue that more attention should be paid to the amateur side of the game, since they are the clubs from which the professionals hail. Meanwhile, the rebuilding of Lansdowne Road continues and much progress is being made. When finished, it will be a 50,000 all-seater stadium. But this season of 2009 will see the Irish home games at Croke Park, and crowds of 80,000 will watch the visitors, England and France.

> **BELOW** Cork Constitution, AIL division one champions, show off the trophy after their 18-8 win over Garryowen in the final at Musgrave Park, Cork.

France: Spirit Burns Hot at Toulouse

by CHRIS THAU

'Newcomers like Maleli Kunavore and Yves Donguy and veterans like Cédric Heymans and Yannick Jauzion all played as if the semi-final … was the match of their lives'

It is difficult to pinpoint with accuracy what makes Stade Toulousain a great club, undoubtedly the most successful in the history of French rugby. It is a melange of factors, objective and subjective, rational and absurd, which have contributed over the years to the creation of the Toulouse legend. A significant factor is the enormous swell of support in the community, reflected in the remarkable public display at the Place du Capitole on Sunday 29 June to celebrate the seventeenth Bouclier de Brennus in the club's 101-year history, as well as the rocklike endorsement of the Amicale de Stade Toulousain, led by former France lock forward, France team manager and hero of the Resistance Henri Foures.

It is money also, generated by the rugby business managed by René Bouscatel but also by the generosity and desire to participate of the local business community, happy to invest millions of Euros in what is universally perceived as their own 'product'.

There is also the ability to produce, hire and retain successful coaching teams of the likes of Skrela and Villepreux of the 1990s, or Guy Novès and his various partners – Daniel Santamans, Serge Laïrle, Philippe Rougé-Thomas and Yannick Bru – over the past decade.

BELOW Champions of France! Jean-Baptiste Elissalde enjoys life as the city of Toulouse turns out to watch its heroes bring home the Bouclier de Brennus.

It is history. The club's Phoenix-like capacity – not unlike other European rugby institutions such as Cardiff, Wasps, Munster, Harlequins, Bayonne, Leicester, Edinburgh and Biarritz – to reinvent itself, to weather the hard times and rebuild successful teams after periods of decline and mediocre return, must be quite significant. This is how Toulouse managed to recapture their edge and winning ways for the intensity of the final stages of the French Championship, having absorbed and digested the defeat in the final of the Heineken Cup only a few weeks earlier.

However, it is the club's ability to recruit, develop and launch virtual unknowns onto the big French and European stage, reshape the careers of others beset by doubts and injury, recast players in new challenging roles and command the loyalty of its veterans that perhaps is the key to its success story. It is the spirit of the game that the club manages to transfer from generation to generation of players, administrators and supporters that enables it to stay what it is.

Newcomers like Maleli Kunavore and Yves Donguy and veterans like Cédric Heymans and Yannick Jauzion all played as if the semi-final against Stade Français was the match of their lives. However, it was the pack of forwards – led by example by skipper Jean Bouilhou and hooker William Servat – tearing into the opposition with such controlled ferocity that left the Parisians without options. Similarly it was the massive team effort – directed with accuracy, cool and control by the duo Byron Kelleher and Jean-Baptiste Elissalde – in the final against eternal challengers Clermont

Auvergne that secured Toulouse *le Bouclier*. Even so, neither the brutal demolition of the Parisians nor the clinical conquest of Clermont could be described in its poetic glory without reference to Toulouse full back Maxime Médard, the 'man of both matches', whose tries at crucial times put the knife into the hearts of both the Parisians and Clermontois. The French media have run out of metaphors to describe the mixture of pace, explosive power and artistry displayed by the 23-year-old. And he has not even yet played for France, though he was the mainstay of the Under 21 French team that won the world title two years ago.

On the other hand, Clermont Auvergne, after a virtually flawless championship campaign that made them hot favourites, failed at their ninth attempt to capture the elusive title. A lover of obfuscatory explanations might have attempted to identify the missing element in obscure factors of a spiritual nature as the team wilted at the last hurdle. There may be some, which require an in-depth analysis that involves both the mental preparation as well as the geometrical accuracy of Vernon Cooper's coaching. But then, as a good and honest Kiwi coach would be prepared to acknowledge, on the day, Clermont were not good enough.

Another significant aspect of this extraordinary French Championship was the return of Toulon Rugby Club to the elite section of French league – and the manner of it. Some three years ago the name Mourad Boudjellal meant very little to your ordinary Stade Mayol regular. At the end of May, after the comprehensive 31-17 win over Racing-Métro 92 that secured the club promotion to the Top 14, the elite division of French professional rugby, the name of the Toulon businessman of Moroccan descent, now club president, was chanted by supporters alongside that of his emblematic right-hand man, Tana Umaga.

The former All Black skipper, who joined the club two years ago as a player, this season became team manager, Boudjellal's agent in the attempt to transform Toulon back into one of the great forces of French rugby. In the aftermath of RWC 2007, he proved instrumental in signing, mostly for one-year contracts, a breathtaking constellation of stars, including Victor Matfield, George Gregan, Andrew Mehrtens, Aaron Mauger and Anton Oliver, who gave sterling service to the club. Mind you, the feeling that this is the United Nations of Rugby, as Toulon have been nicknamed, is strengthened by the presence in the team of Englishman Dan Luger, Czech Martin Jagr, a number of Tongan, Italian and Argentine recruits, and last but not least the team captain, Georgia's Grigol Labadze.

Italy: Calvisano Reach the Top

by CHRIS THAU

'A week after the South African match, Italy ... battled back from a 12-0 deficit to win against Argentina by the narrowest of margins (13-12) in front of 38,000 spectators in Cordoba'

By the middle of May, with the Test against South Africa only a couple of weeks away, Italy head coach Nick Mallett must have been pulling out his hair in despair. With many of his foreign-based stars unavailable for a variety of reasons, ranging from injury to club commitments, and with another batch of 26 players on duty for Italy A in the IRB Nations Cup in Bucharest, his options seemed fairly limited. He must have recalled the 100-point, 15-try romp South Africa had inflicted on the hapless Italians during his own reign as Springbok coach some years ago.

But, as he had no option, in addition to the few regulars available, Mallett boldly went for the in-form players of the leading clubs in the domestic league, as revealed by the final stages of the Italian Championship. The coach's experiment paid off. Although Italy, deprived of more than ten of their first-choice players, lost 26-0 to South Africa in pouring rain at Newlands, Mallett must have felt somewhat pleased by the overall performance of the team. This was the first time the Springboks had failed to score 40 or more points against Italy, and it is the smallest margin in the series since November 1995, when Italy under Georges Costes held the then world champions to a creditable 21-40 final score. Several newcomers made a legitimate statement about their potential, including Luke McLean, Matteo Pratichetti, Gonzalo Garcia, Simon Picone and Ignacio Rouyet.

On the one hand, this may suggest that the quality of Italian domestic rugby is on the way up and that the work of former national coach Georges

Costes, in charge of age-group development, is paying off. This is probably true, as some of the newcomers, including Calvisano hooker and team captain against South Africa Leonardo Ghiraldini, scrum half Picone and winger Pratichetti, as well as the dynamic captain of Italy A, Luigi Ferraro, are products of the elite development programme run by FIR. On the other hand, many of the new players who made an impact in South Africa, like McLean, Rouyet and Garcia, or in Romania, like Manoa Vosawai, are *stranieri* (foreign players), who have become eligible through family links, nationality or residence.

A week after the South African match, Italy, featuring several of the missing stars of the Six Nations campaign – including the brothers Mirco and Mauro Bergamasco, skipper Sergio Parisse and hooker Fabio Ongaro – battled back from a 12-0 deficit to win against Argentina by the narrowest of margins (13-12) in front of 38,000 spectators in Cordoba. A try by replacement hooker Ghiraldini moments from time and Andrea Marcato's conversion plus his two earlier penalties saw Italy nudge ahead of the Pumas' total of four penalty goals in a physical, unspectacular encounter. It was a major achievement against the Pumas, until that afternoon third in the IRB rankings.

Meanwhile, in the final of the Italian league in Monza in front of 8000 spectators, Cammi Calvisano, coached by the Frenchman Marc Delpoux, defeated Benetton Treviso, coached by South African Franco Smith, 20-3, by two tries to none. The new champions had eight *stranieri* in their ranks (McLean, Garcia, Paul Griffen, Aaron Persico, Cameron Treloar, Ben Hand, Ruan Vermeulen and Alistair McKenzie), while Treviso featured 'only' six in Brendan Williams, Benjamin De Jager, Lucas Borges, Marius Goosen, Hottie Louw, and Cornelius Van Zyl. In the semi-finals Benetton, having lost the away leg 16-20, managed to creep through 46-41 on aggregate against Montepaschi Viadana, thanks to a try by Williams in the dying seconds of the home game. In the other semi-final Calvisano, giving a strong signal of intent, despatched Carrera Petrarca Padova, 20-18 at home and 20-13 away.

A Summary of the Season 2007-08

by TERRY COOPER

RUGBY WORLD CUP 2007

POOL A

England	28	USA	10
South Africa	59	Samoa	7
USA	15	Tonga	25
England	0	South Africa	36
Samoa	15	Tonga	19
South Africa	30	Tonga	25
England	44	Samoa	22
Samoa	25	USA	21
England	36	Tonga	20
South Africa	64	USA	15

	P	W	D	L	F	A	BP	Pts
South Africa	4	4	0	0	189	47	3	19
England	4	3	0	1	108	88	2	14
Tonga	4	2	0	2	89	96	1	9
Samoa	4	1	0	3	69	143	1	5
USA	4	0	0	4	61	142	1	1

POOL B

Australia	91	Japan	3
Wales	42	Canada	17
Japan	31	Fiji	35
Wales	20	Australia	32
Fiji	29	Canada	16
Wales	72	Japan	18
Australia	55	Fiji	12
Canada	12	Japan	12
Australia	37	Canada	6
Wales	34	Fiji	38

	P	W	D	L	F	A	BP	Pts
Australia	4	4	0	0	215	41	4	20
Fiji	4	3	0	1	114	136	3	15
Wales	4	2	0	2	168	105	4	12
Japan	4	0	1	3	64	210	1	3
Canada	4	0	1	3	51	120	0	2

POOL C

New Zealand	76	Italy	14
Scotland	56	Portugal	10
Italy	24	Romania	18
New Zealand	108	Portugal	13
Scotland	42	Romania	0
Italy	31	Portugal	5
Scotland	0	New Zealand	40
Romania	14	Portugal	10
New Zealand	85	Romania	8
Scotland	18	Italy	16

	P	W	D	L	F	A	BP	Pts
New Zealand	4	4	0	0	309	35	4	20
Scotland	4	3	0	1	116	66	2	14
Italy	4	2	0	2	85	117	1	9
Romania	4	1	0	3	40	161	1	5
Portugal	4	0	0	4	38	209	1	1

POOL D

France	12	Argentina	17
Ireland	32	Namibia	17
Argentina	33	Georgia	3
Ireland	14	Georgia	10
France	87	Namibia	10
France	25	Ireland	3
Argentina	63	Namibia	3
Georgia	30	Namibia	0
France	64	Georgia	7
Ireland	15	Argentina	30

	P	W	D	L	F	A	BP	Pts
Argentina	4	4	0	0	143	33	2	18
France	4	3	0	1	188	37	3	15
Ireland	4	2	0	2	64	82	1	9
Georgia	4	1	0	3	50	111	1	5
Namibia	4	0	0	4	30	212	0	0

KNOCKOUT STAGES

Quarter-finals

Australia	10	England	12
New Zealand	18	France	20
South Africa	37	Fiji	20
Argentina	19	Scotland	13

Semi-finals

England	14	France	9
South Africa	37	Argentina	13

Third-place Play-off

France	10	Argentina	34

Final

England	6	South Africa	15

INTERNATIONAL RUGBY

ENGLAND TO NEW ZEALAND
JUNE 2008

Opponents	Results
NEW ZEALAND	L 20-37
NEW ZEALAND	L 12-44

Played 2 Lost 2

SCOTLAND TO ARGENTINA
JUNE 2008

Opponents	Results
ARGENTINA	L 15-21
ARGENTINA	W 26-14

Played 2 Won 1 Lost 1

WALES TO SOUTH AFRICA
JUNE 2008

Opponents	Results
SOUTH AFRICA	L 17-43
SOUTH AFRICA	L 21-37

Played 2 Lost 2

IRELAND TO NEW ZEALAND & AUSTRALIA
JUNE 2008

Opponents	Results
NEW ZEALAND	L 11-21
AUSTRALIA	L 12-18

Played 2 Lost 2

FRANCE TO AUSTRALIA
JUNE & JULY 2008

Opponents	Results
AUSTRALIA	L 13-34
AUSTRALIA	L 10-40

Played 2 Lost 2

ITALY TO SOUTH AFRICA AND ARGENTINA
JUNE 2008

Opponents	Results
SOUTH AFRICA	L 0-26
ARGENTINA	W 13-12

Played 2 Won 1 Lost 1

CHURCHILL CUP 2008

(Held in June in USA & Canada)

Pool matches

USA	10	England Saxons	64
Scotland A	26	Canada	10
Scotland A	27	Argentina A	24
USA	9	Ireland A	46
Ireland A	12	England Saxons	34
Argentina A	17	Canada	16

Bowl Final

Canada	26	USA	10

Plate Final

Ireland A	33	Argentina A	8

Cup Final

Scotland A	19	England Saxons	36

ROYAL BANK OF SCOTLAND
SIX NATIONS CHAMPIONSHIP 2008

Results

Ireland	16	Italy	11
England	19	Wales	26
Scotland	6	France	27
Wales	30	Scotland	15
France	26	Ireland	21
Italy	19	England	23
Wales	47	Italy	8
Ireland	34	Scotland	13
France	13	England	24
Ireland	12	Wales	16
Scotland	15	England	9
France	25	Italy	13
Italy	23	Scotland	20
England	33	Ireland	10
Wales	29	France	12

Final table

	P	W	D	L	F	A	PD	Pts
Wales	5	5	0	0	148	66	82	10
England	5	3	0	2	108	83	25	6
France	5	3	0	2	103	93	10	6
Ireland	5	2	0	3	93	99	-6	4
Scotland	5	1	0	4	69	123	-54	2
Italy	5	1	0	4	74	131	-57	2

AUTUMN INTERNATIONAL MATCH 2007

Wales	12	South Africa	34

WORLD CUP WARM-UP MATCHES 2007

England	62	Wales	5
England	15	France	21
Scotland	31	Ireland	21
Wales	27	Argentina	20
France	22	England	9
Italy	36	Japan	12
Ireland	23	Italy	20
Scotland	3	South Africa	27
Wales	7	France	34

UNDER 20 SIX NATIONS 2008

Results

Scotland	6	France	12
Ireland	6	Italy	0
England	28	Wales	15
France	24	Ireland	13

WE'RE BUILT TO LAST

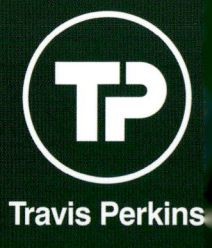

Travis Perkins

EVERYTHING THE TRADE NEEDS TO GET THE JOB DONE

When you choose a builders merchant you want one that's built to last. We've a wealth of experience in the industry, providing a lasting service that's built around your needs including:

- Great service from friendly, knowledgeable staff
- Huge range of building materials available from stock
- Reliable, honest delivery service
- Convenient opening hours

BUILT FOR THE TRADE

www.travisperkins.co.uk

Wales	27	Scotland	10
Italy	13	England	22
Wales	33	Italy	13
Ireland	17	Scotland	12
France	6	England	24
Scotland	15	England	41
Ireland	6	Wales	11
France	26	Italy	14
Wales	20	France	16
Italy	14	Scotland	13
England	43	Ireland	14

Final table

	P	W	D	L	F	A	PD	Pts
England	5	5	0	0	158	63	95	10
Wales	5	4	0	1	106	73	33	8
France	5	3	0	2	84	77	7	6
Ireland	5	2	0	3	56	90	-34	4
Italy	5	1	0	4	54	100	-46	2
Scotland	5	0	0	5	56	111	-55	0

UNDER 18 SIX NATIONS FESTIVAL 2008

(Held in March/April in Cork, Ireland)

Results

England	78	Italy	8
France	8	Scotland	10
Ireland	6	Wales	25
England	18	France	0
Ireland	11	Scotland	25
Italy	10	Wales	43
Ireland	17	Italy	15
Scotland	5	England	32
Wales	25	France	13

Winners: England

IRB JUNIOR WORLD CHAMPIONSHIP 2008

(Held in June in Wales)

Fifth-place Play-off

France	21	Australia	42

Third-place Play-off

Wales	18	South Africa	43

Final

New Zealand	38	England	3

TRI-NATIONS 2008 (to date)

Results

New Zealand	19	South Africa	8
New Zealand	28	South Africa	30
Australia	16	South Africa	9
Australia	34	New Zealand	19
New Zealand	39	Australia	10
South Africa	0	New Zealand	19

IRB PACIFIC NATIONS CUP 2008

Results

Fiji	34	Samoa	17
NZ Maori	20	Tonga	9
Japan	21	Australia A	42
Fiji	7	NZ Maori	11
Samoa	15	Australia A	20
Japan	35	Tonga	13
NZ Maori	17	Samoa	6
Japan	12	Fiji	24
Australia A	90	Tonga	7
Tonga	15	Samoa	20
NZ Maori	65	Japan	22
Australia A	50	Fiji	13
Tonga	27	Fiji	16
Samoa	37	Japan	31
Australia A	18	NZ Maori	21

Champions: NZ Maori

IRB SEVENS WORLD SERIES FINALS 2007-08

Dubai

New Zealand	31	Fiji	21

South Africa (George)

New Zealand	34	Fiji	7

New Zealand (Wellington)

New Zealand	22	Samoa	17

United States (San Diego)

New Zealand	27	South Africa	12

Hong Kong

New Zealand	26	South Africa	12

Australia (Adelaide)

New Zealand	7	South Africa	15

England (Twickenham)

Samoa	19	Fiji	14

Scotland (Murrayfield)

New Zealand	24	England	14

IRB Sevens Champions: New Zealand

WOMEN'S SIX NATIONS 2008

Results

Ireland	19	Italy	0
England	55	Wales	0
Scotland	15	France	43
Italy	6	England	76
Wales	23	Scotland	6
France	26	Ireland	17
Ireland	13	Scotland	3
France	0	England	31
Wales	27	Italy	5
Ireland	10	Wales	19
Scotland	5	England	34
France	35	Italy	6
Wales	3	France	0
England	17	Ireland	7
Italy	31	Scotland	10

Final table

	P	W	D	L	F	A	PD	Pts
England	5	5	0	0	213	18	195	10
Wales	5	4	0	1	72	76	-4	8
France	5	3	0	2	104	72	32	6
Ireland	5	2	0	3	66	65	1	4
Italy	5	1	0	4	48	167	-119	2
Scotland	5	0	0	5	39	144	-105	0

CLUB, COUNTY AND DIVISIONAL RUGBY

ENGLAND (including Anglo-Welsh competitions)

Guinness Premiership

	P	W	D	L	F	A	BP	Pts
Gloucester	22	15	0	7	551	377	14	74
Wasps	22	14	2	6	599	459	10	70
Bath	22	15	0	7	526	387	9	69
Leicester	22	13	0	9	539	428	12	64
Sale	22	14	0	8	481	374	7	63
Harlequins	22	12	0	10	480	440	15	63
London Irish	22	13	0	9	433	382	7	59
Saracens	22	11	0	11	533	525	8	52
Bristol	22	7	1	14	393	473	8	37*
Worcester	22	6	2	14	387	472	8	36
Newcastle	22	7	0	15	333	542	6	34
Leeds	22	2	1	19	336	732	2	12

*Denotes point deducted for fielding an ineligible player

Guinness Premiership Play-offs
Semi-finals

| Wasps | 21 | Bath | 10 |
| Gloucester | 25 | Leicester | 26 |

Final

| Wasps | 26 | Leicester | 16 |

National Leagues
Division One Champions: Northampton
Runners-up: Exeter
Division Two Champions: Otley
Runners-up: Manchester
Division Three (N) Champions: Tynedale
Runners-up: Darlington Mowden Park
Division Three (S) Champions: Mounts Bay
Runners-up: Cinderford

EDF Energy Cup
Semi-finals

| Leicester | 34 | Wasps | 24 |
| Ospreys | 30 | Saracens | 3 |

Final

| Leicester | 6 | Ospreys | 23 |

EDF Energy National Trophy
Quarter-finals

Rotherham Titans	8	Plymouth Albion	19
Bedford Blues	8	Northampton S'ts	32
Exeter Chiefs	42	Esher	7
Nottingham	71	Launceston	3

Semi-finals

| Exeter Chiefs | 16 | Nottingham | 8 |
| Plymouth Albion | 8 | Northampton S'ts | 22 |

Final

| Exeter Chiefs | 13 | Northampton S'ts | 24 |

EDF Energy Intermediate Cup Final
| Birkenhead Park | 18 | Chester | 21 |

EDF Energy Senior Vase Final
| Hartpury College | 83 | Wheatley Hills | 5 |

EDF Energy Junior Vase Final
| Doncaster Phoenix | 11 | Castleford | 14 |

County Championship Final (Bill Beaumont Cup)
| Yorkshire | 33 | Devon | 13 |

County Championship Shield Final
| Northumberland | 25 | Cornwall | 11 |

County Championship Plate Final
| Hampshire | 22 | Leicestershire | 12 |

University Match
| Oxford U | 16 | Cambridge U | 22 |

University U21 Match
| Oxford U | 13 | Cambridge U | 3 |

Women's University Match
| Oxford U | 12 | Cambridge U | 13 |

British Universities Sports Association
Men's Winners: Hartpury College
Women's Winners: UWIC

Inter-Services Champions: The Army

Hospitals Cup Winners: GKT

Middlesex Sevens 2007
Winners: Newcastle
Runners-up: Worcester

Rosslyn Park Schools Sevens
Festival Winners: Cancelled – bad weather
Colts Winners: Brynteg
Junior Winners: RGS High Wycombe
Prep Schools Winners: Abandoned – bad weather
Girls Schools Winners: East Norfolk
Open Winners: Sedbergh

Daily Mail Schools Day
Under 18 Cup Winners: Wellington College
Under 18 Vase Winners: Sussex Downs College
Under 15 Cup Winners: Wellington College
Under 15 Vase Winners: Langley Park

Women's Champions: Saracens
Women's Sevens Champions: Worcester
Ladies Middlesex Club Sevens 2008: Wasps
RFUW Under 18 National Tens: Worcester

<table>
<tr><td>

SCOTLAND

</td><td>

WALES

</td></tr>
</table>

SCOTLAND

Hydro Electric Cup Final
Melrose   31   Heriot's RC   24
Hydro Electric Shield Final
Garnock   31   Kirkcaldy   24
Hydro Electric Bowl Final
Dalziel   10   Preston Lodge   18
Hydro Electric Plate Final
Aberdeen University 27   Portobello   21

Scottish Sevens Winners
Kelso: Selkirk
Selkirk: Selkirk
Gala: Heriot's RC
Melrose: Scottish Thistles
Hawick: Hawick
Berwick: Kelso
Langholm: Newcastle Falcons
Peebles: Watsonians
Earlston: Watsonians
Jed-Forest: Watsonians
Kings of the Sevens: Selkirk

Scotland Hydro Electric Premiership
Division One

	P	W	D	L	F	A	BP	Pts
Boroughmuir	22	20	0	2	659	362	16	96
Watsonians	22	16	0	6	579	431	11	75
Melrose	22	12	1	9	512	374	14	64
Currie	22	12	1	9	482	423	13	63
Ayr	22	11	5	6	359	374	4	58
Heriot's RC	22	11	1	10	498	557	11	57
Stirling County	22	8	3	11	476	495	10	48
Hawick	22	10	0	12	418	567	7	47
Glasgow Hawks	22	7	1	14	409	457	15	45
Edinburgh Acads	22	7	2	13	371	429	9	41
GHA	22	6	3	13	369	462	9	39
Dundee HSFP	22	3	1	18	345	546	11	25

Champions: Boroughmuir
Relegated: GHA, Dundee HSFP

Division Two

	P	W	D	L	F	A	BP	Pts
W of Scotland	22	18	0	4	604	259	12	84
Selkirk	22	19	0	3	535	347	8	84
Biggar	22	16	1	5	578	315	10	76
Haddington	22	12	0	10	501	342	15	63
Jed-Forest	22	12	1	9	406	324	8	58
Stewart's Melville	22	11	0	11	478	474	11	56
Aberdeen GSFP	22	9	1	12	462	418	14	52
Kelso	22	9	0	13	373	474	5	41
Hamilton	22	8	0	14	336	485	8	40
Musselburgh	22	7	0	15	275	596	7	35
Cartha QP	22	6	1	15	385	578	7	33
Hillhead/J'hill	22	3	0	19	267	588	7	19

Champions: West of Scotland
Also promoted: Selkirk
Relegated: Cartha QP, Hillhead/Jordanhill

Division Three Champions: Gala
Runners-up: Peebles

WALES

Konica Minolta Cup
Quarter-finals
Aberavon   32   Ebbw Vale   22
Glam Wanderers   29   Newport   12
Pontypridd   41   Bridgend   11
Cross Keys   28   Neath   44

Semi-finals
Aberavon   10   Pontypridd   33
Glam Wanderers   37   Neath   49

Final
Neath   28   Pontypridd   22

Welsh Premiership

	P	W	D	L	F	A	BP	Pts
Neath	26	19	1	6	697	381	15	93
Cardiff	26	18	1	7	544	449	6	80
Pontypridd	26	16	1	9	523	411	11	77
Swansea	26	16	2	8	547	487	8	76
Ebbw Vale	26	15	2	9	499	430	10	74
Aberavon	26	15	1	10	591	571	10	72
Newport	26	12	0	14	441	462	12	60
Bedwas	26	11	2	13	499	474	12	60
Llanelli	26	10	4	12	527	468	12	60
Glam Wanderers	26	10	2	14	439	451	11	55
Cross Keys	26	10	1	15	430	475	9	51
Bridgend	26	9	1	16	397	515	9	47
Llandovery	26	7	0	19	384	684	5	33
Maesteg	26	4	2	20	415	675	6	26

Welsh Leagues
Division One East

	P	W	D	L	F	A	BP	Pts
Pontypool	22	18	2	2	648	274	13	89
Caerphilly	22	16	2	4	482	316	10	78
Blackwood	22	14	2	6	512	378	11	71
Bargoed	22	14	0	8	538	449	14	70
UWIC	22	13	2	7	554	408	8	64
Llanharan	22	9	1	2	436	442	8	46
Newbridge	22	9	2	11	355	400	5	45
Rumney	22	8	2	12	423	446	8	44
Newport S'cens	22	8	0	14	344	499	5	37
Beddau	22	7	0	15	310	483	6	34
Fleur de Lys	22	5	1	16	300	617	6	28
Llantrisant	22	4	0	18	402	592	10	26

Division One West

	P	W	D	L	F	A	BP	Pts
Tonmawr	22	18	1	3	538	245	12	86
Carmarthen Q	22	17	2	3	553	265	12	84
Narberth	22	17	1	4	566	369	9	79
Merthyr	22	12	0	10	411	378	10	58
Llangennech	22	10	1	11	382	344	11	53
Whitland	22	10	0	12	395	357	8	48
Cwmllynfell	22	11	0	11	335	425	3	47
Bonymaen	22	9	0	13	338	360	8	44
Corus (P Talbot)	22	7	1	14	319	466	7	37
Dunvant	22	8	0	14	288	437	4	36
Bridgend Ath	22	5	1	16	349	482	11	33
Waunarlwydd	22	4	1	17	278	624	2	20

IRELAND

AIB League
Division One

	P	W	D	L	F	A	BP	Pts
Cork Constitution	15	13	1	1	327	133	4	58
Shannon	15	12	0	3	329	177	8	56
Garryowen	15	12	1	2	295	157	5	55
Clontarf	15	10	0	5	285	233	7	47
Blackrock College	15	9	0	6	319	285	7	43
Dolphin	15	9	0	6	269	273	3	39
UL Bohemian	15	7	0	8	252	208	7	35
Old Belvedere	15	6	0	9	307	282	10	34
St Mary's College	15	7	0	8	240	270	5	33
UCD	15	7	0	8	255	337	5	33
Ballymena	15	5	0	10	230	267	7	27
Terenure College	15	4	0	11	228	309	9	25
Dungannon	15	4	1	10	242	309	6	24
Galwegians	15	4	2	9	171	241	3	23
Lansdowne	15	4	1	10	181	280	5	23
Greystones	15	4	0	11	202	371	2	18

Relegated to Division Two: Lansdowne, Greystones

AIB League Play-offs
Division One
Semi-finals

Clontarf	3	Cork Constitution	17
Shannon	6	Garryowen	31

Final

Garryowen	8	Cork Constitution	18

Division Two
Champions: University College Cork
Runners-up: Young Munster

Note: Buccaneers and Young Munster finished the regular season in first and second place respectively in Division Two and were promoted automatically

Division Three
Champions: Instonians
Runners-up: Bruff

Note: Bruff and Instonians finished the regular season in first and second place respectively in Division Three and were promoted automatically

AIB Cup

Blackrock College	9	Shannon	12

AIB Junior Cup

Navan	20	Tullamore	6

Senior Cup Winners
Leinster: Clontarf
Munster: Shannon
Ulster: Belfast Harlequins
Connacht: Galwegians

MAGNERS LEAGUE 2007-08

	P	W	D	L	F	A	BP	Pts
Leinster	18	13	1	4	428	283	7	61
Cardiff Blues	18	12	0	6	395	315	8	56
Munster	18	10	1	7	330	258	6	48
Edinburgh	18	9	3	6	313	285	6	48
Glasgow W'rs	18	10	1	7	340	349	4	46
Llanelli Scarlets	18	7	0	11	403	362	11	39
Ospreys	18	6	1	11	321	255	11	37
Dragons	18	7	1	10	282	394	4	34
Ulster	18	6	1	11	278	407	3	29
Connacht	18	5	1	12	214	396	2	24

FRANCE

'Top 14' Play-offs

Semi-finals

Toulouse	31	Stade Français	13
Clermont Auvergne	21	Perpignan	7

Final

Toulouse	26	Clermont A'gne	20

ITALY

'Super 10'

Final

Benetton Treviso	3	Cammi Calvisano	20

NEW ZEALAND

Air New Zealand Cup 2007

Final

Auckland	23	Wellington	14

Ranfurly Shield holders: Auckland

SOUTH AFRICA

Currie Cup 2007

Final

Free State Cheetahs	20	Golden Lions	18

HEINEKEN CUP 2008

Quarter-finals

London Irish	20	Perpignan	9
Gloucester	3	Munster	16
Saracens	19	Ospreys	10
Toulouse	41	Cardiff Blues	17

Semi-finals

| London Irish | 15 | Toulouse | 21 |
| Saracens | 16 | Munster | 18 |

Final

| Munster | 16 | Toulouse | 13 |

EUROPEAN CHALLENGE CUP 2008

Quarter-finals

Sale	49	Brive	24
Bath	57	Leeds	5
Worcester	36	Montpellier	26
Newcastle	40	Castres	13

Semi-finals

| Worcester | 31 | Newcastle | 16 |
| Bath | 36 | Sale | 14 |

Final

| Bath | 24 | Worcester | 16 |

SUPER 14 TOURNAMENT 2008

Final table

	P	W	D	L	F	A	Pts
Crusaders	13	11	0	2	369	176	52
Waratahs	13	9	1	3	255	186	43
Sharks	13	9	1	3	271	209	42
Hurricanes	13	8	1	4	310	204	41
Stormers	13	8	1	4	269	211	41
Blues	13	8	0	5	354	267	40
Chiefs	13	7	0	6	348	349	34
Force	13	7	0	6	247	278	33
Brumbies	13	6	0	7	277	317	30
Bulls	13	6	0	7	324	347	28
Highlanders	13	3	0	10	257	338	19
Reds	13	3	1	9	258	323	18
Cheetahs	13	1	0	12	255	428	13
Lions	13	2	1	10	206	367	12

Semi-finals

| Crusaders | 33 | Hurricanes | 22 |
| Waratahs | 28 | Sharks | 13 |

Final

| Crusaders | 20 | Waratahs | 12 |

BARBARIANS

Opponents	Results
Combined Services	L 24-27
South Africa	W 22-5
Bedford	W 34-19
Edinburgh Academicals	W 43-0
Belgium XV	W 84-10
Ireland	L 14-39
England	L 14-17

Played 7 Won 4, Lost 3

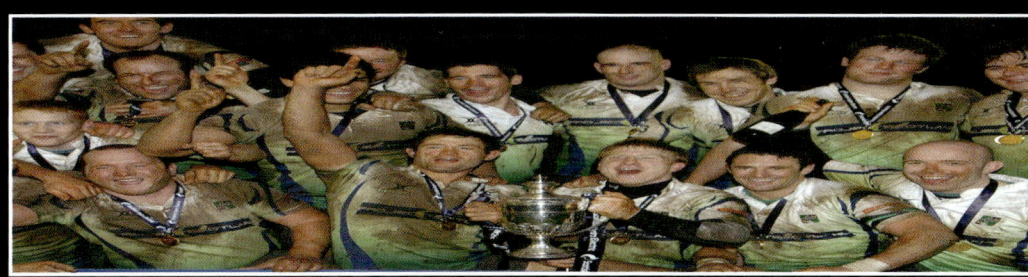

PREVIEW OF THE
SEASON 2008-09

Key Players 2008-09

by IAN ROBERTSON

ENGLAND

JAMES HASKELL

Once RWC 2007 ended, England began planning for the future. The first of the new breed of multi-talented young stars was James Haskell. Initially he took the well-trodden route of England Under 18, Under 19 and Under 21. He was then fast-tracked into the Saxons and in 2007 at the age of only 21 he won a first full cap against Wales in the Six Nations. He could not have had a better mentor at his club, Wasps, than Lawrence Dallaglio and made rapid progress to become the best blind-side flanker in England by the start of the 2008 Six Nations. Standing 6ft 4ins he has developed into a world-class line-out jumper, and at 17½ stone he makes a huge contribution in the ruck and maul. Above all he is an explosive runner, with the perfect combination of raw power and blistering acceleration. Not only is he dynamic with the ball in hand, he is also outstanding at the breakdown and fiercely effective in defence. He is already a special player who will only get better with more experience and is destined to be in the England team for the long haul. He will surely make the Lions squad to South Africa in 2009.

DANNY CIPRIANI

There's always an air of excitement when a brilliant young fly half bursts onto the scene, and there can be no doubt that Danny Cipriani was a prodigiously talented 20-year-old when he made his first Test start against Ireland at Twickenham in 2008. The fact that Jonny Wilkinson was dropped for him in this match sums up the huge potential the Wasps player has. Last season was his first full year of Premiership rugby and he was almost a victim of his own versatility, switching from fly half to full back and looking quite capable of filling in anywhere in the threequarter line. Blessed with electric acceleration and genuine speed – he is as fast as Paul Sackey – he is an elusive runner with an eagle eye for a gap who can slice through the best of defences. He kicks well off either foot and is a very good goal-kicker. He is a strong defensive player and reads the game well. He is likely to be the star of the England team through to the next World Cup and beyond, although he has to recover from a dreadful ankle injury sustained in mid-May. If he is fit for the Six Nations, he looks a shoo-in for the 2009 Lions.

SCOTLAND

ALASDAIR STROKOSCH

It is an interesting fact that in good times and bad Scotland always seem to have a full complement of top-notch back-row forwards. From the days 20 years ago of Finlay Calder, Derek White, John Jeffrey and Jim Calder, right through to the current crop of Ali Hogg, Simon Taylor and Jason White, there has always been stiff competition for places. Add to the list the name of Alasdair Strokosch. He has emerged in the past couple of years to reach international status after following a rather circuitous route. He began playing club rugby for East Kilbride and Boroughmuir before starting his professional career with Edinburgh, where he first came to prominence, producing consistently good peformances and showing great potential. He made his mark with the Scotland Sevens side and won Scotland A caps before earning his first full cap against Australia in 2006. He joined Gloucester and benefited enormously from the intensity of playing in the Guinness Premiership and Europe. He is an extremely powerful back-row forward who bulldozes into the opposition to make the hard yards. He is also an aggressive defensive player who is in his element round the rucks and mauls. A good scrummager, he brings real ballast to the pack and is just the sort of physical player the Scots need.

CHRIS PATERSON

In February 2008 Chris Paterson became Scotland's most-capped back when he won his 83rd cap to overtake Gregor Townsend, going on to become Scotland's most-capped player overall when he won his 88th cap against Argentina in Buenos Aires that June. Scotland won this Test and he produced a man-of-the-match performance. Between his debut against Spain in the 1999 World Cup and the end of the 2007-08 season, he had scored a record 687 points for Scotland, 20 points more than the previous holder – Gavin Hastings. He has also written his name further into the record books with a remarkable run of 36 consecutive successful kicks at goal for Scotland between August 2007 and June 2008, in the process slotting every single attempt in the World Cup and the 2008 Six Nations Championship. His golden run ended when he missed with his thirty-seventh shot in the first Test

against Argentina in Rosario on 7 June 2008. Of course, he is far more than a great goal-kicker. He is equally effective at full back, fly half or wing and is a deadly attacking footballer. With 22 tries to his name, he is only two behind the Scottish record held by Ian Smith and Tony Stanger. Apart from a recent brief spell with Gloucester, he has been the mainstay of the Edinburgh team. His wealth of experience is so important to Scotland.

WALES

MARTYN WILLIAMS

Martyn Williams is one of the few players to have shown that despite the ferocious physicality of modern professional rugby it is still possible to have a long career. He played his first international for Wales against France in September 1996, and 12 seasons later he is still an established fixture and automatic first choice at open-side flanker in the Welsh team. He has now won 81 caps and scored 73 points for Wales. He announced his retirement from international rugby after Wales failed to reach the quarter-finals of the 2007 World Cup, but when Warren Gatland was appointed the new Wales coach shortly afterwards he was persuaded to make himself available once again for the national team. He is an outstanding back-row forward and is just as important to Wales as Richie McCaw is to the All Blacks. He was a key player when Wales won the Grand Slam in 2005 and he was just as influential when they repeated those heroics in 2008, scoring in the final match against France in Cardiff. He is a brilliant support player with great hands and has the instinctive running skills of a threequarter. He is outstanding at the breakdown and is also a hugely competitive defensive player. A natural leader, his huge experience is invaluable to the Welsh team.

SHANE WILLIAMS

In the modern professional era with the players becoming bigger and stronger every year, it is very encouraging that a will-o'-the-wisp wing like Shane Williams can not only survive but really flourish. He is without question one of the best and most exciting wings in the world game, and he has come a long way since winning his first cap in 1999-2000. At that time he was only 22 years old and weighed about 11 stone. He has filled out since then but would still be one of the lightest wing threequarters in international rugby – just over half the weight of Jonah Lomu in his prime. He scored his first try for Wales against Italy in the 2000 Six Nations Championship and by the end of the 2008 season he had become Wales's top try scorer of all time with 43, having overtaken the record set by Gareth Thomas. He played a major part in helping Wales collect the Grand Slam in 2005, scoring three tries,

one each against Italy, Scotland and England, and toured with the Lions to New Zealand, scoring five tries in the midweek match against Manawatu. He enjoyed a second Grand Slam with Wales in 2008, scoring two tries against both Scotland and Italy and one each against Ireland and France. He is blessed with blistering pace and tears defences apart with his twinkletoed sidestepping.

IRELAND

DENIS LEAMY

Like several Irish international rugby players, Denis Leamy began his sporting career with hurling. He switched schools at the age of 15 and played rugby at centre for Rockwell College, playing in the Munster Cup in his first year in the school team. By the time he left school, he was playing in the back row and it is as a No. 8 or flanker that he has made the transition to the Irish international team. He first sprang to prominence when he was picked to play for Munster, the top Irish province for the past few years, Declan Kidney (the new Irish coach for the 2008-09 season) selecting him when he was only 19 years old. In 2003 he signed a full-time professional contract with Munster and was a major force as they won the Heineken Cup twice in three years, beating first Biarritz in the 2006 final, then Toulouse in 2008. He first appeared for the full Ireland team in 2004 against the USA, playing at open-side flanker, the position he also occupied against Italy in his first Six Nations game. However, he soon reverted to No. 8, where he featured in the Irish Triple Crown team of 2006, although he played four games at blind-side in the 2008 competition. He is an aggressive, powerful player who is ruthless in defence and a strong runner with the ball in attack.

EOIN REDDAN

Eoin Reddan began his representative career with Munster, but the hugely successful Irish province was not short of scrum halves, with Peter Stringer their regular first choice. In 2005 Reddan left Munster to join Wasps and settled in quickly. At the start he was number two behind then England international Matt Dawson, but not only did he get regular game time, he was also able to tap into Dawson's vast experience. There is no doubt that Reddan has benefited greatly from the club's great success during the past three seasons and it is no coincidence he impressed quickly behind a back row of Tom Rees, Lawrence Dallaglio and James Haskell and alongside a fly half as good as Danny Cipriani. With the retirement of Dawson, he is now number one at Wasps and also with Ireland. He won his first cap against France in the Six Nations in 2006, and the following year he played in Ireland's

final two pool games at the 2007 Rugby World Cup. In 2008 he featured in all five of Ireland's Six Nations games, winning the man-of-the-match award against Italy. He is a very quick, accurate passer of the ball. He is sharp on the break and kicks and defends well. He should now establish himself in the Irish team.

FRANCE

THIERRY DUSAUTOIR

Thierry Dusautoir is the latest in a long line of great French back-row forwards. He had to serve an extended apprenticeship before winning his first full cap for France, but he has very quickly established himself in the team. He began his senior career at Bordeaux Bègles but then joined Biarritz and appeared in the 2006 Heineken Cup final, which they lost 23-19 to Munster at the Millennium Stadium. Shortly after that match, Dusautoir made his Test debut against Romania in Bucharest, scoring his first try for France in their 62-14 victory. His next Test came a week later at Newlands in Cape Town when France beat South Africa 36-26. He joined Toulouse in 2006-07 and suffered his second Heineken Cup final defeat, once again against Munster, in May 2008. By then, he had become a regular in the back row for France. Having taken part in their 2007 World Cup warm-up matches, he was a first-choice flanker in the tournament itself, playing in the wins over Namibia and Ireland in the pool matches and in the great victory over the All Blacks in the quarter-finals. He is very fast, has great hands, is very good at the breakdown and is a great tackler.

JEAN-BAPTISTE ELISSALDE

The French team has had an inconsistent few years often underperforming in the big matches. The main problem has been the failure to marry up a top-class pair of half backs to operate behind a pretty effective pack of forwards. On far too many occasions the mercurial Frédéric Michalak has let France down in the crucial crunch matches. He looks brilliant against average opposition, but he doesn't cut the mustard at the highest level. Now there is a real possibility that Jean-Baptiste Elissalde could solve this long-term problem. The question is whether to pick him at fly half or scrum half because he looks to be equally comfortable playing in either position. He began as a fly half with La Rochelle but in 2002 moved to Toulouse, where he came up against Michalak and switched to scrum half. He is a good passer of the ball and is very powerful on the break. He kicks well and is tactically astute as well as being strong and confident in defence. He has spent the past four years in competition with Dimitri Yachvili for the scrum-half place in the French side, but he now seems happy to revert to playing fly half again. An excellent goal-kicker, he helped France win the Grand Slam in 2004 and could just solve their half-back problem in 2009.

ITALY

CARLOS NIETO

In the nine short years since Italy first joined what became, with their inclusion, the Six Nations Championship, they have made a great deal of progress. In particular they have produced a thoroughly decent set of forwards year after year so that one of Italian rugby's great strengths has become the solid platform they enjoy in the scrummage area on their own ball and an ability on the opposition ball to make life very difficult for their opponents. In particular they have come up with a consistently formidable front three, the current incumbents comprising arguably the best front row in world rugby. The two Italian props, Martin Castrogiovanni and Carlos Nieto, are both world class, and the latter is all things to all men when it comes to prop forwards. He is outstanding at the set piece and asks all sorts of questions of his opposite number. He is also a really good support player at the line out and is quick to add his considerable weight and strength to the rucks and mauls. Even though they finished bottom of the table in the 2008 Six Nations, Italy are definitely closing the gap and their front row have certainly played their part.

ANDREA MARCATO

The real problem for Italian rugby in the past few years has been that behind a well-organised, strong set of forwards they have had only two or three backs of the highest quality. They were fortunate when they first joined the Six Nations in that they had a great fly half in Diego Dominguez and a top scrum half in Alessandro Troncon. Now they have retired, the focus of attention is Mirco Bergamasco. He is a world-class centre, but the rest of the backs cannot match his exploits. The new hope is Andrea Marcato. Having made his debut against Japan in 2006 but without really establishing himself, he burst onto the scene in the 2008 Six Nations Championship. He most certainly looked a cut above the other Italian backs, and new Italy coach Nick Mallett must be delighted he has such a talented individual to work with. Firstly, Mallett must decide on Marcato's best position. He is quick, a very good

ball player and an elusive runner. He kicks and tackles consistently. With the experience of only a handful of caps, he landed a last-minute dropped goal to enable Italy to beat Scotland in Rome and in the summer converted Leonardo Ghiraldini's last-gasp try to bring Italy victory in Argentina. He would have more of an influence if he switched from full back to fly half.

Fixtures 2008-09

AUGUST 2008

Sat. 16th	Middlesex Sevens (Twickenham)
Sat. 30th	English National League 1
	Scottish Prem/ship 1-3
	Scottish Nat. Leagues 1-3
	Welsh Nat. Leagues E & W 1

SEPTEMBER 2008

Fri. 5th	Magners Celtic League (1)
Sat. 6th	English National Leagues 1-3
	EDF Senior Vase (1)
	EDF Junior Vase (1)
	Scottish Prem/ship 1-3
	Scottish Nat. Leagues 1-3
	Welsh Principality Premiership
	Welsh Nat. Leagues E & W 1
Sat 6th and Sun. 7th	Guinness English Premiership
Tue. 9th	Magners Celtic League (5) (2 matches brought forward)
Fri. 12th	Magners Celtic League (2)
Fri. 12th to Sun. 14th	Guinness English Premiership
Sat. 13th	English National Leagues 1-3
	Scottish Prem/ship 1-3
	Scottish Nat. Leagues 1-3
	Welsh Principality Premiership
	Welsh Nat. Leagues E & W 1
Fri. 19th	Magners Celtic League (3)
Fri. 19th to Sun. 21st	Guinness English Premiership
Sat. 20th	Help for Heroes XV v International Select XV (Twickenham)
	English National Leagues 1-3
	Scottish Prem/ship 1-3
	Scottish Nat. Leagues 1-3
	Welsh Principality Premiership
	Welsh Nat. Leagues E & W 1
Fri. 26th	Magners Celtic League (4)
Fri. 26th and Sat. 27th	Guinness English Premiership
Sat. 27th	English National Leagues 1-3
	EDF Senior Vase (2)
	EDF Junior Vase (2)
	Scottish Prem/ship 1-3
	Scottish Nat. Leagues 1-3
	Welsh Principality Premiership
	Welsh Nat. Leagues E & W 1
	Welsh Swalec Cup (1)

OCTOBER 2008

Wed. 1st	Guinness English Premiership
Fri. 3rd	Magners Celtic League (5)
Fri. 3rd to Sun. 5th	EDF Energy Cup (1)
Sat. 4th	English National Leagues 1-3
	Scottish Prem/ship 1-3
	Scottish Nat. Leagues 1-3
	Welsh Principality Premiership
	Welsh Nat. Leagues E & W 1
	AIB Irish Leagues 1-3
Thu. 9th	European Challenge Cup (1) (1 match)
Fri. 10th to Sun. 12th	Heineken Cup (1)
	European Challenge Cup (1)
Sat. 11th	English National Leagues 1-3
	Scottish Prem/ship 1-3
	Scottish Nat. Leagues 1-3
	Welsh Principality Premiership
	Welsh Nat. Leagues E & W 1
	AIB Irish League 3
Sat. 11th and Sun. 12th	AIB Irish Leagues 1, 2
Thu. 16th	European Challenge Cup (2) (1 match)
Fri. 17th to Sun 19th	Heineken Cup (2)
	European Challenge Cup (2)
Sat. 18th	English National Leagues 1, 2
	EDF National Trophy (1)
	EDF Intermediate Cup (1)
	EDF Senior Vase (3)
	EDF Junior Vase (3)
	Scottish Prem/ship 1-3
	Scottish Nat. Leagues 1-3
	Welsh Principality Premiership
	Welsh Nat. Leagues E & W 1
	AIB Irish Leagues 1-3
Fri. 24th	Magners Celtic League (6) (3 matches)
Fri. 24th to Sun. 26th	EDF Energy Cup (2)
Sat. 25th	English National Leagues 1-3
	Scottish Prem/ship 1-3
	Scottish Nat. Leagues 1-3
	Welsh Principality Premiership
	Welsh Nat. Leagues E & W 1
	Welsh Swalec Cup (2)
	AIB Irish Leagues 1-3
Fri. 31st Oct to Sun. 2nd Nov.	EDF Energy Cup (3)

NOVEMBER 2008

Sat. 1st	English National Leagues 1-3
	Scottish Prem/ship 1-3
	Scottish Nat. Leagues 1-3
	Welsh Principality Premiership
	Welsh Nat. Leagues E & W 1
Tue. 4th	Barbarians v Combined Services (Plymouth)

Sat. 8th — ENGLAND v PACIFIC ISLANDS
WALES v SOUTH AFRICA
IRELAND v CANADA
FRANCE v ARGENTINA
ITALY v AUSTRALIA
English National Leagues 1-3
Welsh Principality Premiership

Fri. 14th to
Sun. 16th — Guinness English Premiership
Sat. 15th — ENGLAND v AUSTRALIA
IRELAND v NEW ZEALAND
SCOTLAND v SOUTH AFRICA
WALES v CANADA
ITALY v ARGENTINA
English National Leagues 1-3
Welsh Principality Premiership
Welsh Swalec Cup (3)
Welsh Swalec Bowl (1)

Tue. 18th — Munster v New Zealand
Fri. 21st to
Sun. 23rd — Guinness English Premiership
Sat. 22nd — ENGLAND v SOUTH AFRICA
IRELAND v ARGENTINA
SCOTLAND v CANADA
WALES v NEW ZEALAND
FRANCE v AUSTRALIA
English National Leagues 1
EDF National Trophy (2)
EDF Intermediate Cup (2)
EDF Senior Vase (4)
EDF Junior Vase (4)

Tue. 25th — Welsh Principality Premiership
Fri. 28th — Magners Celtic League (7)
Fri. 28th to
Sun. 30th — Guinness English Premiership
Sat. 29th — WALES v AUSTRALIA
Scottish Prem/ship 1-3
Scottish Nat. Leagues 1-3
AIB Irish Leagues 1-3

DECEMBER 2008

Wed. 3rd — Barbarians v Australia
  (Wembley)
Thu. 4th — European Challenge Cup (3)
  (1 match)

Fri. 5th to
Sun. 7th — Heineken Cup (3)
European Challenge Cup (3)
Sat. 6th — Barbarians v South Africa
  (Twickenham) (TBC)
English National Leagues 1-3
Scottish Prem/ship 1-3
Scottish Nat. Leagues 1-3
Welsh Principality Premiership
Welsh Nat. Leagues E & W 1
AIB Irish Leagues 1-3

Thu. 11th — Oxford U v Cambridge U
  (Twickenham)
European Challenge Cup (4)
  (1 match)

Fri. 12th to
Sun. 14th — Heineken Cup (4)

Sat. 13th — European Challenge Cup (4)
English National League 1
EDF National Trophy (3)
EDF Intermediate Cup (3)
EDF Senior Vase (5)
EDF Junior Vase (5)
Scottish Prem/ship 1-3
Scottish Nat. Leagues 1-3
Welsh Principality Premiership
Welsh Nat. Leagues E & W 1
AIB Irish League 3

Sat. 13th and
Sun. 14th — AIB Irish Leagues 1, 2
Fri. 19th — Magners Celtic League (6)
  (delayed)
Sat. 20th — English National Leagues 1-3
Scottish Prem/ship 1-3
Scottish Nat. Leagues 1-3
Welsh Swalec Cup (4)
Welsh Swalec Bowl (2)
Welsh Swalec Plate (1)

Sat 20th and
Sun. 21st — Guinness English Premiership
Fri. 26th — Magners Celtic League (8)
Fri. 26th and
Sat. 27th — Guinness English Premiership
Sat. 27th — English National League 1
Welsh Principality Premiership
Welsh Nat. Leagues E & W 1

JANUARY 2009

Thu. 1st — Welsh Principality Premiership
Fri. 2nd — Magners Celtic League (9)
Sat. 3rd — English National Leagues 1-3
Welsh Principality Premiership
Welsh Nat. Leagues E & W 1

Sat. 3rd and
Sun. 4th — Guinness English Premiership
Fri. 9th — Magners Celtic League (10)
Fri. 9th to
Sun. 11th — Guinness English Premiership
Sat. 10th — English National Leagues 1-3
Scottish Prem/ship 1-3
Scottish Cups (1)
Welsh Principality Premiership
Welsh Nat. Leagues E & W 1

Fri. 16th to
Sun. 18th — Heineken Cup (5)
European Challenge Cup (5)
Sat. 17th — EDF National Trophy (4)
EDF Intermediate Cup (4)
EDF Senior Vase (6)
EDF Junior Vase (6)
Scottish Prem/ship 1-3
Scottish Nat. Leagues 1-3
Welsh Principality Premiership
Welsh Nat. Leagues E & W 1
AIB Irish Leagues 1-3

Fri. 23rd to
Sun. 25th — Heineken Cup (6)
European Challenge Cup (6)
Sat. 24th — English National Leagues 1-3

	Scottish Prem/ship 1-3
	Scottish Nat. Leagues 1-3
	Welsh Swalec Cup (5)
	Welsh Swalec Bowl (3)
	Welsh Swalec Plate (2)
	AIB Irish Leagues 1-3
Sat. 31st	English National Leagues 1–3
	Scottish Prem/ship 1-3
	Scottish Nat. Leagues 1-3
	Welsh Principality Premiership
	Welsh Nat. Leagues E & W 1
	AIB Irish Leagues 1-3

FEBRUARY 2009

Sat. 7th	ENGLAND v ITALY
	(Twickenham, 15:00)
	IRELAND v FRANCE
	(Croke Park, 17:00)
	English National League 3
	EDF National Trophy (5)
	EDF Intermediate Cup (5)
	EDF Senior Vase (7)
	EDF Junior Vase (7)
	Scottish Prem/ship 1-3
	Scottish Nat. Leagues 1-3
Sun. 8th	SCOTLAND v WALES
	(Murrayfield, 15:00)
Tue. 10th	Welsh Principality Premiership
Fri. 13th to	
Sun. 15th	Guinness English Premiership
Sat. 14th	FRANCE v SCOTLAND
	(Stade de France, 16:00)
	WALES v ENGLAND
	(Millennium Stadium, 17:30)
	English National Leagues 1-3
Sun. 15th	ITALY v IRELAND
	(Stadio Flaminio, 15:30)
Fri. 20th	Magners Celtic League (11)
Fri. 20th to	
Sun. 22nd	Guinness English Premiership
Sat. 21st	English National Leagues 1-3
	Scottish Prem/ship 1-3
	Scottish Nat. Leagues 1-3
	Scottish Cups (2)
	Welsh Swalec Cup (6)
	Welsh Swalec Bowl (4)
	Welsh Swalec Plate (3)
	AIB Irish Leagues 1-3
Fri. 27th	FRANCE v WALES
	(Stade de France, 21:00)
Sat. 28th	SCOTLAND v ITALY
	(Murrayfield, 15:00)
	IRELAND v ENGLAND
	(Croke Park, 17:30)
Sat. 28th and	
Sun. Mar. 1st	Guinness English Premiership
	English National League 3
	EDF National Trophy Q- finals
	EDF Intermediate Cup Q-finals
	EDF Senior Vase Quarter-finals
	EDF Junior Vase Quarter-finals
	Welsh Principality Premiership

MARCH 2009

Fri. 6th	Magners Celtic League (12)
Fri. 6th to	
Sun. 8th	Guinness English Premiership
Sat. 7th	English National Leagues 1-3
	Scottish Prem/ship 1-3
	Scottish Nat. Leagues 1-3
	Welsh Principality Premiership
	Welsh Nat. Leagues E & W 1
	AIB Irish Leagues 2, 3
Sat. 7th and	
Sun. 8th	AIB Irish League 1
Fri. 13th to	
Sun 15th	Guinness English Premiership
Sat. 14th	ITALY v WALES
	(Stadio Flaminio, 16:00)
	SCOTLAND v IRELAND
	(Murrayfield, 17:00)
	English National League 1
Sun. 15th	ENGLAND v FRANCE
	(Twickenham, 15:00)
Wed. 18th	Barbarians v Bedford Blues
Sat. 21st	ITALY v FRANCE
	(Stadio Flaminio, 14:15)
	ENGLAND v SCOTLAND
	(Twickenham, 15:30)
	WALES v IRELAND
	(Millennium Stadium, 17:30)
Sat. 21st and	
Sun. 22nd	Guinness English Premiership
	English National Leagues 2, 3
	EDF National Trophy Semi-finals
	EDF Intermediate Cup S-finals
	EDF Senior Vase Semi-finals
	EDF Junior Vase Semi-finals
Fri. 27th	Magners Celtic League (13)
Fri. 27th to	
Sun. 29th	Guinness English Premiership
	EDF Energy Cup Semi-finals
Sat. 28th	English National Leagues 1-3
	Scottish Prem/ship 1-3
	Scottish Nat. Leagues 1-3
	Welsh Nat. Leagues E & W 1
	Welsh Swalec Cup – Q-finals
	Welsh Swalec Bowl – Q-finals
	Welsh Swalec Plate – Q-finals
	AIB Irish Leagues 1-3

APRIL 2009

Fri. 3rd	Magners Celtic League (14)
Sat. 4th	English National Leagues 1-3
	Scottish Cups (3)
	Welsh Principality Premiership
	Welsh Nat. Leagues E & W 1
	National U20s Ch/ship Q-fs
Sat 4th and	
Sun. 5th	Guinness English Premiership
Tue. 7th	Barbarians v Blackheath
Fri. 10th to	
Sun. 12th	Heineken Cup Quarter-finals
	European Challenge Cup Q-fs
Sat. 11th	English National Leagues 1

	Welsh Principality Premiership
	Welsh Nat. Leagues E & W 1
	AIB Irish Leagues 1-3
Fri. 17th	Magners Celtic League (15)
Fri. 17th to	
Sun. 19th	Guinness English Premiership
Sat. 18th	EDF Energy Cup Final
	EDF National Trophy Final
	EDF Intermediate Cup Final
	English National Leagues 2, 3
	Scottish Cups Quarter-finals
	Welsh Principality Premiership
	Welsh Nat. Leagues E & W 1
	Welsh Swalec Cup Semi-Finals
	Welsh Swalec Bowl Semi-finals
	Welsh Swalec Plate Semi-finals
	AIB Irish Leagues 1-3
	National U20s Ch/ship S-finals
Fri. 24th	Magners Celtic League (16)
Sat. 25th	Guinness English Premiership
	English National Leagues 1-3
	English National 3 Play-off
	Scottish Cups Semi-finals
	Welsh Principality Premiership
	Welsh Nat. Leagues E & W 1

MAY 2009

Fri. 1st to	
Sun. 3rd	Heineken Cup Semi-finals
	European Challenge Cup S-fs
Sat. 2nd	County Championship Plate (1)
	Welsh Principality Premiership
Fri. 8th	Magners Celtic League (17)
Sat. 9th	Guinness Premiership S-finals
	EDF Senior Vase Final
	EDF Junior Vase Final
	Bill Beaumont Cup (1)
	County Championship Shield (1)
	County Championship Plate (2)
	Scottish Cups - Finals
	Welsh Swalec Cup Final
	Welsh Swalec Bowl Final
	Welsh Swalec Plate Final
	National U20s Ch/ship Final

Fri. 15th	Magners Celtic League (18)
Sat. 16th	Guinness Premiership Final
	Bill Beaumont Cup (2)
	County Championship Shield (2)
	County Championship Plate (3)
Sat. 23rd	Bill Beaumont Cup (3)
	County Championship Shield (3)
	County Ch/ship Plate S-finals
Sat. 23rd and	
Sun. 24th	Heineken Cup Final
	(Murrayfield)
	European Challenge Cup Final
Sat. 30th	Bill Beaumont Cup Final
	County Ch/ship Shield Final
	County Ch/ship Plate Final

BRITISH & IRISH LIONS IN SOUTH AFRICA 2009

Sat. 30th May	Highveld XV v Lions (Royal Bafokeng, Rustenberg)
Wed. 3rd Jun.	Golden Lions v Lions (Johannesburg)
Sat. 6th Jun.	Cheetahs v Lions (Bloemfontein)
Wed. 10th Jun.	Sharks v Lions (Durban)
Sat. 13th Jun.	W Province v Lions (Cape Town)
Thu. 18th Jun.	Coastal XV v Lions (Port Elizabeth)
Sat. 20th Jun.	SOUTH AFRICA V LIONS (Durban)
Tue. 23rd Jun.	Emerging Springboks v Lions (Cape Town)
Sat. 27th Jun.	SOUTH AFRICA V LIONS (Pretoria)
Sat. 4th Jul.	SOUTH AFRICA V LIONS (Johannesburg)

Wooden Spoon
ANNIVERSARY

Mission Statement

Wooden Spoon aims to enhance the quality and
prospect of life for children and young persons in the
United Kingdom who are presently disadvantaged either
physically, mentally or socially

Charity Registration No: 326691

THE SPORTING CLUB

PROUD SUPPORTERS OF WOODEN SPOON

"GOOD FOOD IN A RELAXING ATMOSPHERE, WITH SUPERB AFTER DINNER SPEAKERS"

Now in its eighteenth year, the Sporting Club is one of the leading providers of Sporting Dinners in the UK. The principal objective of Sporting Club Dinners is to provide members with the environment in which to entertain clients, colleagues or friends in pleasant surroundings with excellent speakers from the World of Sport.

The Clubs	Venues
Capital	The London Marriott, Grosvenor Square
East Midlands	East Midlands Conference Centre
Gloucestershire	Hatherley Manor Hotel, Gloucester
Leeds	The Leeds Marriott
Manchester	The Ramada Piccadilly
North Worcestershire	Worcester Rugby Club
Solihull	St John's Hotel, Solihull
South Staffordshire	The Molineux, Wolverhampton F C
South Warwickshire	Warwick Hilton, Warwick
Sutton Coldfield	Moor Hall Hotel & Spa
West Country	Marriott Hotel, Bristol

Previous speakers have included:-

Sports	Sporting Speakers
Rugby	Jason Leonard OBE, Gareth Edwards, Will Greenwood MBE
Cricket	Shane Warne, Dickie Bird MBE, Ian Botham OBE
Snooker	Steve Davis OBE, John Parrott MBE, Denis Taylor
Football	Sir Geoff Hurst, Jack Charlton OBE, Matt Le Tissier
Boxing	Sir Henry Cooper, Alan Minter, Frank Bruno
Others	Sir Stirling Moss, Sir Ranulph Fiennes, Roger Black MBE

If you wish to attend a Sporting Club Dinner please contact
David Trick
Telephone: 01373 830720   Facsimile: 01373 830999
Email - david@sportingclubgroup.com

Or Visit www.sportingclubgroup.com for further details

The Sporting Club (UK) Ltd, P O Box 3582, Laverton, Bath, BA2 7ZR